A John Wain Selection

Longman Imprint Books

General Editor: Michael Marland

Titles in the series

Companion cassettes, with readings of some of the key stories, are available for the following:

LONGMAN IMPRINT BOOKS

A John Wain Selection

ten short stories, together with a selection of poems and extracts from two novels by

John Wain

With a specially written introduction by the author

editor
Geoffrey Halson M.A.
Head of the English Department, Hounsdown School

This book is accompanied by a cassette recording of John Wain reading *Goodnight, Old Daisy,* and *Manhood*

Longman

LONGMAN GROUP LIMITED
London
Associated companies, branches and representatives
throughout the world

© *John Wain 1958, 1960, 1963, 1964, 1966, 1967, and 1969*
This edition © *John Wain 1977*

This edition first published by Longman Group Ltd 1977

ISBN 0 582 23328 3

Printed in Hong Kong by
Hong Kong Printing Press Ltd

The Life Guard first appeared in "Playboy" magazine
Manhood first appeared in "Ladies Home Journal"
A Message from the Pig-Man first appeared in "Everywoman"
The Valentine Generation first appeared in "Argosy"
Christmas at Rillingham's first appeared in "Suspense"
Rafferty first appeared in "Esquire"
Goodnight, Old Daisy first appeared in "Argosy"
King Caliban first appeared in the "Saturday Evening Post"
I Love You Ricky first appeared in "The Listener"
Down Our Way first appeared in "The Reporter"

Contents

Contents

An Introduction for Student Readers

Many thousands of students must, over the past few years, have been particularly moved by reading John Wain's short story, "A Message From The Pig-Man". They may have gone on to read more of John Wain's short stories, perhaps "Nuncle and other stories" (his first collection and available in Penguin) or "Death of the Hind Legs and other stories" (also available in Penguin). This *Longman Imprint* is, however, the first student edition of John Wain's stories. The ten stories in this *Imprint* illustrate the very varied range of John Wain's fiction. For readers who like to study thematic relationships between stories, the stories are presented here in a deliberate order.

The first three stories, in their different ways, each reveal the preoccupation of certain characters with physical strength. In the title story, "The Life Guard", Jimmy wants to prove himself as Life Guard to visitors at the seedy little resort of Red Rocks by staging a heroic mock rescue, using his old acquaintance Hopper as the victim. In "Manhood", Mr Willison equates the achievement of manhood with the possession of athletic prowess and pushes his unwilling son, Rob, into a rigorous diet of cycling, football and boxing. In "King Caliban", Bert seeks to turn his mentally weak but physically strong brother Fred into a wrestler for purely materialistic motives.

The next two stories in the collection, "I Love You, Ricky" and "Christmas At Rillingham's", both have as their backgrounds the world of pop music. "I Love You, Ricky" tells of the rivalry of two of Ricky's teenage fans, Elizabeth and Hilda, over the possession of a cufflink snatched from Ricky in the scrimmage following one his concerts, whilst "Christmas At Rillingham's" is set in a record shop where the voluptuous young assistant, Patty, draws in the local teenagers to buy pop records under the approving gaze of Mr Rillingham.

"Rafferty" and "The Valentine Generation" explore contrasting aspects of being in love. Isobel, on the rebound from a passionate affair with Rafferty, is being propositioned by a very persistent young man, Walter, who uneasily believes that Isobel is still in love with Rafferty. In "The Valentine Generation", a girl who has just posted a very angry letter to her boyfriend and has immediately regretted it, tries to persuade the postman emptying the letterbox to give the letter back to her.

The last three stories all involve special problems in human relationships, in particular problems of communication and integration. In "A Message from the Pig-Man", the six-year-old boy Ekky is trying to cope with his parents' divorce, his father's leaving home, and his mother's remarriage, problems which defy explanation in his child's world. "Down Our Way" is a disturbing story of how an ostensibly religious family accidentally acquires a coloured lodger and reveals that very worst type of racial prejudice which stems from self-righteousness. In "Goodnight, Old Daisy", the elderly Mr Greely spends every day at a local collection of railway relics, where the major exhibit is the old steam locomotive that he used to drive. He is isolated in his fantasy world, reliving in his mind the great days on the footplate.

I hope that this selection of John Wain's writing, and his own Introduction that follows, will encourage student readers to discover more of his work. Some of his poems are included after the stories, and sections from two of his novels which are particularly attractive for following up these stories.

Geoffrey Halson

About These Stories

an introduction by John Wain

Every time I sit down to write a short story I take particular delight in two things: that it is a story, and that it is short.

This sounds like a feeble attempt at a joke but actually I'm serious. Story-telling or, to call it by its formal literary name, fictional narrative is a very enjoyable art, both for the producer and the consumer. It is one of the ways in which we can express our sense of the richness and unexpectedness of life. To write stories, or to read them, is never a waste of time, so long as the story has some truth to life.

But, you may say, if truth to life is what we're after, why not tell about things that actually happened? Well, there is a place for that too, of course. The real-life story is interesting, or boring, in exactly the same way that life itself is interesting or boring. And, in the end, it doesn't give either the teller or the listener much freedom to manoeuvre. If somebody tells you a story that really happened – one that he can vouch for, or produce evidence for – all you can do is listen. It happened, and whatever comment you make won't alter that fact. And neither can he alter it, except by departing from the facts as he knows them. He can tell the story well or badly, but in the end there is very little he can do to put his individual mark on it. If it is improbable (and some pretty improbable things *do* happen, by the operation of mere chance) all you can do is just accept it. But in an invented story, the reader and the writer start fair. The writer is saying, "I will tell you a story about something that might have happened, illustrating the way people are likely to behave." And the unspoken appeal to the reader is, "That's the kind of thing that happens, isn't it? This is what the human being is like, or don't you agree?" The reader, in his turn (or the hearer, if the story is spoken and not written), can give his own reaction, can believe it or disbelieve it – using the word not in the sense of "believing it actually happened" but "believing that the world is like that, and that people of the kind described, put into the situation that the writer imagines, would behave in that way". The writer is not trying to deceive the reader; on the contrary, he is trying to share with the reader his view of the world.

So, to come back to my first sentence, I take a delight in the fact that a story *is* a story, that it is made up and not "true". What about the other half of the definition? What about the "short"?

Narrative is of many kinds. There is a way of telling a story that is natural to face-to-face narration, where the story-teller can gesticulate, alter his voice to indicate different speakers, put on an accent, indicate his own feelings by his tone of voice, and so on. There is a way of telling a story that is natural to cold print, where everything must be very precisely in the words, which are to be read in silence and translated into the reader's mind in terms of sound and movement. There is a halfway house which is natural to theatre. (A playwright sits in his study and writes a play, but it is the actors and actresses and the director and the scene designer who actually get the story across to the audience.) There is a way that is natural to film. There is a way that is natural to television. Or to the ballad, or the puppet-show, or any other way of telling a story that you can think of.

Now, within the realm of literary narrative – stories written down and intended to be read by an individual reader sitting by himself – the two main categories are the novel and the short story. Superficially they may look alike, because they are both invented stories and they are both handed to the reader in printed form. Actually they are as different as chalk and cheese, as I have discovered in twenty years of practising both.

Story-telling is primarily an exercise of imaginative insight. It depends on the ability to put oneself in other people's places, and imagine what their lives are like and how they think and feel. (At least, realistic story-telling does, the kind I aim at and which is aimed at in all the stories in this book. Fantasies of the Godzilla-Meets-the-Wolf-Man type, exploiting nightmare and insecurity, are something else again, and so is Noddy and Big-Ears.) This kind of imaginative insight is not confined to writers, of course. It is something we all need, something without which it is impossible to hold down any responsible job or deal with people effectively at any level. But the writer practises it professionally and all the time. You can get quite a good idea of the kind of thinking a writer has to do if you keep your eyes open and your imagination busy in ordinary life. Sit in a bus, watch the people who get on and off (stealthily, of course – it is rude to stare) and try to imagine the background of their lives and what kind of people they are. An ugly man gets on; with him is a pretty girl who is obviously in love with him. What on earth does she see in him? An old lady gets on; what was she like as a young girl, fifty years ago? That man in a frayed raincoat talking to himself, is he a harmless crank or a potential murderer? And what made him like that? We can't, of course, know the answers to all these questions, but we can make plausible guesses. And notice, please, that they are the kind of guesses we are forced to make all the time, whether we want to or not, in our dealings with people. We shall never understand them unless we can get inside their heads and discover what makes them tick, and thus put ourselves in a position to predict their reactions to what we do and say. Politicians, businessmen, teachers, administrators, are all using this kind of shrewd guesswork all the time, and so are you and I.

In a novel, it is essential to imagine the characters (or at any rate, the principal characters) in considerable depth. Which means in practice that it is impossible to write a novel about people who do not bear some resemblance to you, the writer, if not in temperament, then at least in background and circumstances. For instance, if I were to try to write a novel about a coal-miner, I should be handicapped by the fact that I do not know any coal-miners, have never lived in a mining community, or even been down a mine, and would be guessing from the outside. I could, of course, take lodgings in a mining village, try to get to know some miners, arrange to go down to the coal-face, and all the rest of it. But such "research" tends to lie on the surface instead of being really worked into the soil. And at the end of it, if I succeeded in getting to know some miners really well, I should only be at the starting-point; all the problems of the novel would still remain to be solved. It is simpler to write about the kind of people I already know well, whose lives I can imagine from hour to hour because I know what kind of work they do, in what surroundings, what they talk to each other about, what they do in their leisure, etc. These, in my own case, happen to be the professional middle class, people like doctors, lawyers, journalists, teachers, and those connected with the arts such as musicians, painters, writers and actors. These are the people I mix with and among whom I naturally belong. And since the experiences of such people are real experiences – they are born and die and fall in love and suffer and enjoy and have adventures and fall ill and die, as much as anyone else – there is no reason why they should not be as good material for a novel as speed cops or deep-sea divers.

When I write novels, then, I put in the centre of a story a character, or cluster of characters, belonging to the type I know best, the type to which, making due allowance for individual differences, I belong myself. Other, very different, characters may come into the story; they may be very prominent in it; but the focal point has to be the perceiving eye of someone I feel I can understand. For instance, in a novel of mine called *A Winter in the Hills*, one of the principle characters is a mountain-bred Welshman, the owner-driver of a tiny bus service which is struggling to avoid being taken over by a bigger concern. I portray this man at full length, imagining his life and background from childhood to middle age, and he is certainly not based on anyone I know. But I could not get away with trying to tell the story from his point of view. The perceiving eye is that of the central character (the "hero", to use an old-fashioned term that still has its usefulness), who is an Englishman of very much my own background and generation. Since the Welsh bus driver is portrayed chiefly in terms of how he seems to the hero, it is possible for me to get close enough to write about him.

Now, in the short story it is possible to throw this kind of caution to the winds. I may not know any miners, but I can stand next to a miner at the bar of a pub, and chat with him for a while or hear him talking to his mates, and I can have, suddenly, the feeling that I know what it is like to be he. Not always, not over long stretches, but now, at this moment. The short story, which does not call for a lot of detail but merely for the telling arrangement of a brush-stroke here and there, can allow the writer to portray, even if only in snapshot fashion, lives that are largely mysterious to him. Thus I find that in the stories collected here I have imagined what it is like to be a strong, slow-witted man who is talked into becoming an all-in wrestler; a young girl with an adolescent crush on a pop-singer; a lad in a dead-end job who gets his own back on his employer by a practical joke; a child with separated parents; a retired engine-driver; a kindly and sentimental postman; and various others. None of these are characters I could have written a whole novel about. The background material, the detail in which I am able to imagine their lives, would have dried up after a couple of chapters. But they are all people whom I feel confident of understanding at that particular point in their lives.

So there it is. You, the reader, and I, the writer, start fair, because none of these stories "really happened". What I am offering you is my notion of the way human beings behave. Given the circumstances I imagine them in, given the kind of people I think they are, this is how they react, how they think and feel and talk to one another. How about it? Are these good guesses? Or could you do better? Read the stories, test your guesses against mine – and above all, have fun: because a story that you don't enjoy will never start your imagination working.

JOHN WAIN

The Life Guard

"Hey, see that one go by?" said Hopper. He leaned forward, staring with all his might through the window of the hut. "The tall one in the white bathing dress?"

"Yes," said Jimmy. He flicked a few times with a duster at the clean paintwork.

"The dress was too small for her, did you notice?" said Hopper. "You could see plenty. *Plenty*."

"I don't give much thought to it."

"Of course, you must get so used to it, it's boring," said Hopper. "You get your chances here, all right."

"I don't give much thought to it."

"All day and every day," said Hopper. He went to the door, opened it and stared after the girl in the white bathing dress. "I'll wait till she starts sunbathing, then I'll go and look her over."

"Suit yourself," said Jimmy.

Nobody knew why Hopper was called Hopper. It was neither his surname nor his Christian name. But he had been called Hopper at school, as far back as Jimmy could remember, and he could remember back to pretty well their first day there, at the age of five. And now Hopper was an apprentice and Jimmy was the Life Guard of Red Rocks. Everybody was growing up.

"Girls," said Hopper. "They're all waiting for it. Just waiting for it, they are. I soon found that out, at our place."

"There's all sorts," said Jimmy vaguely. He was beginning to tire of the conversation.

"Nah, there's only one sort," said Hopper. He shot Jimmy a crafty look from under his pimply forehead. "They don't think about anything but boys. They sit around thinking about it till they do half your work for you."

"How d'you mean, half your work?"

"When you start to soften 'em up," said Hopper in a quiet, husky voice. He gave a quick glance over each shoulder, as if afraid someone would come into the hut and overhear him. "You find they've been thinking about it so much, they're half-way there already." He winked and gave a quiet snigger.

1

"I think I'll have a swim," said Jimmy. He began to take off his shirt.

"Give the birds a look at that manly torso of yours," said Hopper. "You get a good tan, doing this job."

Jimmy wished that Hopper would not examine him so closely. He took his trousers off and hung them neatly over the back of one of the hut's two chairs.

"Swimming trunks on already," said Hopper.

"What else?" Jimmy asked. "I've a job to do."

"Oh, do me a favour," said Hopper. He sniggered again. "Your job is to walk around and make the birds feel good. You'll never have to rescue anybody."

"I'm going swimming now," said Jimmy. "I have to keep in practice."

"I'm not stopping you," said Hopper.

"Yes, but the hut," said Jimmy. "I have to leave it empty. It's a regulation."

Hopper stopped looking cunning and looked sulky. "You mean nobody's allowed in the hut?"

"Not without me," said Jimmy.

Hopper got to his feet. "What kind of a regulation is that?" he asked.

"One of Mr Prendergast's."

"Oh, *him*."

"He's my boss," said Jimmy. He watched Hopper out and then closed the door of the hut. "Why don't you come in swimming if you want something to do?" he asked.

"I've got something to do. I'm going to find that girl in the bathing dress that's too small for her and see if there's anything doing."

They parted, Jimmy towards the sea and Hopper along the beach. As he walked briskly towards the water, Jimmy thought briefly about Hopper and the girl. He was quite certain that when Hopper located her he would never have the nerve to go up and speak to her. He would just sit himself down, about twenty-five yards away, and look at her and think his thoughts. Hopper had always talked about girls in that way, from the time he was eleven years old, but really he was very shy with them. At least as shy as Jimmy himself, which was saying a lot. Since he had left Red Rocks and gone to be an apprentice in an engineering works, and only came home at weekends and holidays, Hopper had talked about girls more than ever, but Jimmy did not believe the things he said. He knew that Hopper had picked up all those stories from listening to the other apprentices. Hopper would never find a girl to do all those things with; he was thin and flat-chested, he had greasy hair that came down so close to his eyebrows that there was hardly room for his pimples, he had bad teeth, and he was not even clever.

The waves came creaming along the sand towards Jimmy's feet. The day was overcast but not at all cold, and the sea looked green and lush as a meadow. Jimmy ran forward until the water was up to his knees, then dived under and began to swim with strong, easy strokes.

Red Rocks is a struggling little place. Also straggling. A long road leads down to the sea, running straight across the sandhills because there are no trees and nothing to turn aside for, and along this road there are a few houses, some in clusters as if afraid of the loneliness, a few bigger ones sturdily on their own. There is also the High Hat Ballroom, which used to be the Rialto Cinema, and there is Owen's Fish and Chip Saloon. Further up, at the T-junction, there is the older and more settled part of the village. Fifty or sixty houses, two pubs and a red-brick church.

For a hundred years or more, Red Rocks has been trying to establish itself as a summer resort. It has the clean, salt sea, it has fresh Atlantic air, and in the little bay it has a half-circle of smooth pale sand, as elegantly rounded as a child's cuticle. At the northern edge of the bay rises the cluster of rocks that gives the place its name, high enough and rough enough for the adventurous big boys of fourteen and fifteen to climb and shout to one another and feel that they're really climbing something. Yes, the place has the makings of a resort. But no more than the makings. A few visitors come in August, a little shanty town of caravans and tents grows up in the field behind Owen's Fish and Chips, but at the beginning of September it all dies down again. Once that cold wind starts whipping across the sandhills, nobody wants to come near the place. And even in the short season of hot weather, when the sea winks in the sunlight and the rocks feel warm to your hand, most visitors go to the larger resorts down the coast, where there are more amenities. Red Rocks keeps in business by holding prices down, offering simple food and not too many amusements to burn up the hard-earned sixpences that have been put by. The families who take their holidays there are usually lower-income-bracket.

Most people in Red Rocks were pretty well resigned to these facts before Mr Prendergast came. In fact, some of them positively liked things the way they were. The pushing, enterprising young ones had all gone off to the towns anyway, and the older ones liked a quiet life. Even some of the young people found it not too bad. Jimmy Townsend, for instance. You wouldn't have said that anything could worry Jimmy, a strongly built boy with a round face and not too much up top. Most of Jimmy's life, except for the tiresome interruptions of morning and afternoon school, was spent either bicycling or swimming. He would have liked to be a P.T. instructor, but that was just the trouble, you had to have training for that, and to get the training you had to pass your exams and go on a special course, and Jimmy could never get on well enough at school to pass any exams. He just couldn't give his mind to it. So when he turned fifteen he just left school and hung about at home. There wasn't any work to do. Sometimes, in the afternoons, he helped out with a bit of potato-peeling for Mr Owen, or dug the Vicar's garden, but it was a rare week when he earned more than ten shillings, and with his big appetite it cost more than that to feed him for a day. After six months of this, it was clear that the time was coming when Jimmy would have to go away to one of the nearby big towns, and live in a hostel and get a job. And this was what worried him. He didn't want to go away. He liked Red Rocks even in the winter, when the salty wind made his eyes fill with tears and sometimes made him get off his bicycle and push it, against the wind's great roaring weight, down the road to the beach. Even the short, dull winter days, when the cold fog lay still on the water, and all you could hear was the muffled rattle of waves pushing the shingle about, and sometimes the cry of a sea-bird, suited him. Jimmy had plenty of patience; he knew how to wait. He would lean on his bicycle and look at the sea and reckon up how many weeks would have to pass, before he could go swimming.

Swimming was Jimmy's great happiness. He could do any stroke. His arms were so powerful, his big chest held so much air, the salty sting of the water sent his blood racing so fast, that he felt more fully alive in the water than on land. Mr Rogers, the school-master, had made jokes about it. "One of the larger mammals reversing the evolutionary process," he used to say of Jimmy. "Townsend is evolving backwards into a marine animal. If he has offspring, they'll probably be gill-breathers." And he called Jimmy the Amphibian, taking care to explain the derivation from two Greek works so as to make his joke educational for the class.

Jimmy didn't know what reversing the evolutionary process was, but he took it all in good part and waited for school to end so that he could go swimming. And when he got too old to go to school he went swimming more than ever, to get away from his worried feeling. Even on a winter day he would take a plunge if it wasn't too freezing cold, moving rapidly through the water for ten or fifteen minutes before running out and towelling himself in the lee of the rocks. A seal, people said. He ought to come back to earth next time as a seal. But his father grumbled about the cost of keeping him at hime, and his mother said nothing but set her lips and began to make enquiries about a nice hostel for clean-living boys in Barrow-in-Furness or Fleetwood or even as far away as Preston. No wonder Jimmy worried. In a place like that, there would be no sea, no rocks, no sand. He would have to spend all the week working, and do his swimming on crowded Saturday afternoons in municipal baths that stank of chlorine.

That was where Mr Prendergast stepped in, with his Development Group. Mr Prendergast really changed Jimmy's life. He was a young and forceful man in rimless glasses who had opened a pharmacy in Red Rocks to sell sun-tan lotion and denture powder to the visitors, and he wanted a lot more customers. He was always talking about Changing the Image. Red Rocks would begin to thrive straight away if it could only Change its Image. He formed a Development Group because he despaired, and quite rightly, of getting any action out of the old Rural District Council.

One evening Mr Prendergast was over in Morecambe and he got talking to a man in the lounge bar of an hotel. This man told him that visitors stayed away from Red Rocks because the bathing was dangerous. Mr Prendergast pooh-poohed the notion, but the man said that there were dangerous currents that swept people out into the Atlantic. This had happened to three people in one season – about 1920, the man thought – and the fact had been widely mentioned in the newspapers. Ever since then, Red Rocks had been known to everyone in the north-west as a place where it was unsafe to bathe.

Mr Prendergast, his glasses flashing angrily, continued to insist that the idea was preposterous and that Red Rocks was a bather's paradise, and he parted on bad terms with his informant. But as he drove home through the night, he worried about this important part of the Image. It nagged at him all the way home, and just as he was turning into his own gateway he got the answer. A Life Guard. A brawny life-saver to be on duty on the beach every day during the season, and not to leave his post until the last bather had gone. He could have a little hut to keep his things in, and to shelter in when it rained, and the hut could have a flag flying above it with a conspicuous colour and the words "Life Guard". As he stopped the engine and got out of his car, Mr Prendergast even knew who the Life Guard would be and how much, or how little, they could get him for. That Jimmy Townsend – he and the job were made for each other. What a piece of luck!

The other members of the Development Group, when Mr Prendergast told them his idea at the next meeting, made only one stipulation: that Jimmy Townsend should go and get a diploma in the approved methods of life-saving. So Jimmy went to Morecambe and took some tests. He swam better than the people who were testing him and got his diploma the first time. The hut was built in June. There was a little delay in getting the flag with the words "Life Guard" on it, so Jimmy's mother embroidered one, and Jimmy fixed it up on a pole himself. Everybody said it looked very nice, and Mr Prendergast and his Group sent out a brochure which mentioned "Excellent Bathing for all the Family. Fully Qualified Life Guard and Swimming Instructor Permanently in Attendance".

Jimmy's father was annoyed at that, and said that if he was going to give swimming lessons to every Tom, Dick and Harry that chose to ask for them, as well as being Life Guard, he ought to get two wage-packets. But Mr Prendergast said it would keep Jimmy from getting bored, because the bay was perfectly safe and there would be nothing for him to do as Life Guard.

All through that summer, the sea danced for joy and Jimmy swam like a glistening porpoise. He practised until he could stay under water for a minute at a time, and when he broke the surface and came blinking up into the sunshine, water poured off his sleek head and the gulls wheeled and cried as if they had seen a walrus. Wading back for a rest, he felt the sand suddenly warm beneath his feet where the water ended, and the red rocks glowed all June under the hot blue of the sky. In the early summer, nobody came to the beach except at week-ends, so for five days on end Jimmy was lord and owner of the sea and the shore, king of birds, master of crabs, director of shells and seaweed. At the highest point to which the tide reached, there was an irregular line of oddments – dried seaweed, shells, corks, salt-whitened sticks, and man-made rubbish – which the tide had carelessly pushed in front of it and abandoned. This line of innumerable weightless objects stretched out as far as you could see on either side, away down the beach, and Jimmy could imagine it going round the whole of England, Scotland and Wales. Every twelve hours the sea came in and inspected this casual demarcation line, nudging it here and there, straightening one section and pushing the next into a curve. It was not only the sea's frontier, it was Jimmy's. He knew that it would only last for the summer; in winter, the furious high waves would come streaming in and the harmless little objects would be flung far inland, to be scattered by the wind. But for the summer, it was something Jimmy could share with the kind of sparkling sea. Every time he crossed that line, going towards the water, he felt his troubles fall away from him and was conscious of nothing but the strength and springiness of his body. And every time he crossed it coming out, with his face towards the straggling village and the sand dunes, he felt wariness gather round him like a wet towel.

Not that there seemed to be anything he need be wary of. Mr Prendergast, on behalf of the Development Group, gave him his small wage, every Saturday night, and seemed quite satisfied with the bargain. He did nothing to interfere with the arrangements, beyond coming down to the hut one Saturday morning and tacking a typewritten notice on it. The notice was in capital letters and was protected from the weather by a sheet of transparent plastic. It announced that swimming lessons would be given free of charge on application to the Life Guard. Jimmy was pleased to see himself referred to, in capital letters, as the Life Guard, and he smiled at Mr Prendergast.

"Give the people any help they seem to want, Jimmy," said Mr Prendergast, looking seriously at Jimmy through his glasses. He was a stout, unsmiling young man and his fair hair was thinning out. What remained was caught by the breeze and fluttered gaily as he spoke. "Bring them into it. Specially the shy ones. Keep a look out for the ones who look lonely and go up and talk to them. Ask them if they want a swimming lesson."

"Yes, sir," said Jimmy. "If they can't swim here they never will. The water's lovely."

"I must try it myself one day," said Mr Prendergast, turning to walk back to his car. Personally he preferred to give his energy

7

to thinking of ways of increasing his income. Swimming was all right for animals that lived in the water. "If I ever do," he added, "I'll make sure that you're all ready to save me if I get out of my depth." He chuckled good-humouredly and Jimmy produced an answering chuckle.

"Well, keep at it," said Mr Prendergast. "Not that there seems to be much to keep at," he added as he moved away.

"The sea's always there, sir," said Jimmy quickly.

"Yes," Mr Prendergast agreed. "Even if the bathers aren't."

He clambered up the rough stone steps and got into his car. Jimmy felt slightly anxious as he went back into the hut. He hoped Mr Prendergast would not begin to regret that he had made him Life Guard and Swimming Instructor. He looked through the window of the hut: it was ten o'clock and the first visitors were just arriving with their beach balls and picnic baskets. He must find someone among this lot, or among one of these lots one of these days, who wanted to be taught to swim. Or, better still, needed to have their life saved.

Time melted away, between joy and anxiety. Now it was August. The field behind Owen's Fish and Chips held three straggling rows of caravans, from little ones like hen-coops on wheels to immense silvery ones fit to be called Mobile Homes. And in the corners of the field, hiding from the wind behind the thick, sloping hedges, were little rashes of tents, holding their heads up above the trampled grass like clusters of mushrooms. It was high season and the weather was good, so that when all the younger visitors crowded together into the High Hat Ballroom or queued for Owen's Fish and Chips, you would have thought that Red Rocks was a thriving resort at last. But even now the boarding houses were only half full.

One Saturday morning, Jimmy managed to get into conversation with a fat woman who was sitting on the beach by herself. He could see that she had a bathing costume and towel with her and he asked her if she liked swimming. The fat woman said that she liked bathing but she couldn't swim. She just splashed about. This was Jimmy's opportunity and he at once offered to teach her to swim. Two or three lessons, he said, and she'd be swimming and then she need never fear getting out of her depth. The fat woman said that she never went out of her depth anyway, and she was too old to start learning to swim now. Jimmy privately agreed with this, but he persisted. There were quite a lot of people on the beach that morning and it would be good publicity if they saw him teaching somebody to swim. So he shifted from one foot to the other and bent over the fat woman as she sat on the sand, and said that bathing was much more fun if you could swim, and doctors all said how good swimming was for you, and the lessons would be free of charge. "I'm paid by the Development Group," he urged. "It's free service to visitors."

He felt a fool, bending over the fat woman, and it annoyed him to see out of the corner of his eye that Hopper was standing a few yards away, watching him and grinning. With Hopper was his younger sister, a scrawny girl of ten or eleven with her hair in a pony-tail. Her name was Agnes and she was always making fun of someone or something. Jimmy had never heard her voice except raised in mockery. He did not remember ever hearing her say anything in a normal tone.

Blushing, he turned his back on Hopper and Agnes, and continued to press the fat woman to let him teach her to swim. It was a sultry day; there was a grey haze over the sea and the sun glared down through a hot mist. Jimmy felt himself sweating.

"I'll just start you off," he said to the fat woman. "Then you can carry on and practise by yourself till you feel ready to go on to the next stage."

To his surprise, the fat woman suddenly gave in and agreed to let him start her off. She gathered up her things and went off to one of the bathing huts to get changed. Jimmy stood waiting, his arms crossed on his chest, trying to look grave and responsible. But he could not help being aware that Hopper and Agnes were coming towards him and Agnes was giggling.

"Is that the best you can do, then?" Hopper asked, grinning and jerking his thumb in the direction of the fat woman. "There's some good-lookers here today. Be a pleasure to hold them up in the water."

"Jimmy's too shy for that," said Agnes in a high affected voice. "He's frightened of girls, everybody knows that."

"She wants to learn to swim," said Jimmy off-handedly.

"Come off it," said Hopper. "She wants to get near a nice young feller and it's her only chance to."

"Jimmy's her last chance," said Agnes. "Last chance Jimmy, last chance Jimmy, oh, oh, oh," she sang to the tune of "If you knew Susie".

"If she starts drowning will you rescue her?" Hopper jeered. "I bet she'd like that. Ow, hold me tight, I'm going under," he mimed the fat woman, holding out his arms and writhing to and fro.

"It's too hot to argue," said Jimmy.

"The water'll rise when she gets in," said Hopper. "High tide'll be two hours early."

"Jimmy picked the fattest one on purpose," said Agnes. "He can hide behind her so the girls can't see him in his little briefs."

Jimmy longed for the fat woman to come back. Then he saw her approaching. She wore a flowered one-piece bathing costume and a rubber cap. Her thighs brushed together as she walked. Everything about her was thick and white.

"Here she comes," said Hopper. "Two-Ton Tessie. Get the lifeboat out."

"Right then," Jimmy greeted the fat woman. He smiled at her. She looked nervous. "Let's just get in and get used to the water first," he said.

"It's the first time I've bathed this year," she said tensely.

"You'll find the water very nice," said Jimmy.

"Last chance Jimmy, last chance Jimmy," Agnes sang in the background. "Oh, oh, oh."

Jimmy and the fat woman walked towards the sea. "We'll just do a nice easy breast-stroke," he said to her. It embarrassed him slightly to say the word "breast" to a woman. He kept his eyes carefully to the front. The thundery air seemed to be pressing down on his forehead. When they reached the water, Jimmy ran ahead and lightly ducked below the surface. The fat woman advanced step by laborious step, letting the water creep up her pale thighs. "It's cold, isn't it?" she said plaintively. Finally she sank to her knees, with the water at waist-level, and stayed there.

"Well, here's the first exercise," said Jimmy. "What we do, we take the legs first." He showed her how to rest her palms on the sea-floor and hold her chin up while doing a simple frog-like movement with her legs.

But the fat woman was hopeless. She got down as if she meant to do some press-ups, but she seemed unable to move her legs, and every time a tiny wave splashed round her chin she gasped and threw her head up like a frightened mare.

"Look, kick your legs like this, nice and easy," Jimmy urged.

"I'd rather learn at the baths," she puffed.

"You'll soon get confidence," said Jimmy. He sat down on the sea-bottom, with his head and shoulders out of the water, and looked at her helplessly. He felt sure everyone must be watching them and laughing. Ought he to get hold of the fat woman's legs and show her the movements? He just did not know. Perhaps that was what real swimming instructors did: but the fat woman's legs looked so white and pulpy that to touch them seemed obscene.

They splashed about for another five minutes, getting nowhere at all, and then the fat woman said she was cold and was going to get out and dress. Jimmy splashed by her side and they walked up the beach together with water pouring down their legs and arms.

"You'll soon get the hang of it," he said to her, smiling so that the people could see.

"I'll never swim the Channel, that I do know," she said.

She went off to dress and Jimmy towelled himself inside the hut. The door opened and there were the grinning faces of Hopper and Agnes.

"Hey, you stopped too soon," said Hopper. "She was just getting in the mood."

"Jimmy was frightened even of *her*," said Agnes. Her narrowed eyes were as green as a cat's. She put out her tongue and it was like a thin, poisonous wafer.

"Kindly get out of my hut," said Jimmy, swinging round to face them. Agnes disappeared at once, but Hopper stayed where he was and said, "You used to be able to take a joke."

Jimmy looked out of the window. The beach was fairly full but it could have been much fuller. The sea was a wonderful cool refuge from the sticky, headachy day but there were only a couple of dozen people splashing about in it. At the big resorts, they would be jostling one another in the sea, stepping over each other on the beach. Suddenly he felt as Mr Prendergast must feel. It was just not working. Next summer the Life Guard's hut would be taken down and he, Jimmy, would be sent off to the city and shut up all week in an engineering works. He felt desperate.

"Hopper," he said, "come in and shut the door."

Hopper obeyed. "Want a private talk?" he said. "Don't say anything I might regret."

"I want you to do something for me," said Jimmy. "Stage a little demonstration." His heart was thumping heavily.

"A demonstration what of?" Hopper asked.

"Life-saving."

"I don't know anything about life-saving."

"No," said Jimmy. "But I do."

He had dried himself by now and he began to put his clothes

on, turning his back to Hopper. But he could feel Hopper watching him. When he turned round, dressed, Hopper's eyes were small and calculating.

"A fake rescue?" he said.

"No fake. I know how to rescue people and I'd like a chance to show what I can do."

"You've got a certificate, isn't that enough?"

"It isn't. I want to pull off a good big rescue at a crowded time like Saturday or Sunday afternoon, right where everyone can see it. Then they'll know the bathing is safe."

"How will they know the bathing's safe if someone pretends to be drowning?"

"They'll see me rescue him. Then they'll know they're being looked after."

"I see," said Hopper slowly. "Nobody wants to learn to swim, so you want somebody to get into trouble and get rescued so everybody'll see you're a big shot."

"Not somebody. You. I want you to go in swimming, pretend to get into trouble, wave to me and give a shout, and I'll swim out and tow you back to shore."

"What d'you think I am, daft?"

"It'll be no trouble, the whole thing'll be over in ten minutes, and I don't expect you to do it for nothing. There's five quid in it for you."

"Not enough," said Hopper.

"It's more than I earn in a week."

"That's your problem. If I'm going to look a fool in front of everybody, the kind of fool that goes out swimming and can't stay in his depth, I want ten quid at least."

"Ten...? You won't look a fool, it might happen to anybody to get caught up in a dangerous current."

"It might, but it doesn't. I'd be the first and I'd look a fool. I need five pounds for doing the job and another five for looking a fool, in front of birds and all. You're lucky I don't make it fifteen."

"You'll do it then?"

Hopper paused for a long moment and then he said, "Cash down first."

"I can't give you cash down. I haven't got it – I'll have to save it up and it'll take me the whole season."

"How much have you got?"

"Three-ten."

"Right, give me that and an IOU for the rest."

He tore a page from his notebook and showed Jimmy how to write out an IOU. "You've got to pay me now," he said. "I can take you to court if you don't. And what about the three-ten?"

"I've got it at home. You can have it tonight."

"Right."

"But you must do the job tomorrow afternoon."

"Right."

Jimmy waited a long time on Sunday afternoon before Hopper came down the road and on to the beach. Hopper was carrying a towel but no bathing costume.

"Are you ready to go in?"

"Yes," said Hopper. "Don't be so anxious. I've got my trunks on under my clothes. Let me come in the hut and change."

"You'd better go to one of the cubicles like everyone else. It'll look funny if you don't."

"All right."

Changed, Hopper looked thin, a pathetic land animal with small blue veins in his legs.

"Let's get it over," he said, shivering already in the cool breeze.

"I've got it worked out," said Jimmy. "We'll go in together and swim out till I say. Then we'll stop and I'll swim back to the shore. You wait a bit, then go out a bit further, and when you're not too close to anyone else, wave your arm and shout for help. I don't want anyone else rescuing you."

"No," said Hopper, "else they'd have to give me ten quid too, wouldn't they?"

He grinned derisively, then looked miserable again. "Oh, let's get it over. I hate the bloody sea."

"You do bathe sometimes. I've seen you."

"Well, I wasn't going to bathe today, so let's get it over."

They walked into the sea, pretending to chat like two friends. When the water came up to waist-level, Jimmy got down and began to swim.

"Come on," he said.

"It's cold," said Hopper sourly. He stood with the water lapping his bathing shorts, as if he was beginning to have second thoughts about the whole thing.

Jimmy swam round him in a circle. "Come on, think of the ten quid."

"That's safe anyway. I've got your IOU."

"But you wouldn't," said Jimmy. "You wouldn't be a rotten cheat."

"What are you being? Faking a rescue."

"It's not a fake. It's a demonstration. If you don't do it I shan't give you the ten quid and I don't care what they do to me."

Hopper suddenly flopped into the water and began to swim slowly and clumsily. Jimmy swam beside him at the same pace. They went on in silence for a few minutes and then Jimmy said, "Right, stop."

Hopper let his feet down to the bottom and stood on them. The water came up to his nipples.

"A bit further on," said Jimmy.

"No," said Hopper. "This is as far out as I'm going."

"Don't be silly. You can't look as if you're in trouble when you've got your head and shoulders out of the water."

"Well," said Hopper. He considered. "I'll wait here while you go back to the shore and then I'll swim a bit further out and call for help from there."

"All right," said Jimmy. "Only do a good job. Think of the ten quid."

"I ought to have said twenty."

Without answering, Jimmy swam back to the shore and stood up with his feet still in the water. Folding his arms, he walked up and down for a few moments, swivelling his head and body in a leisurely, graceful way so as to survey the whole scene. He conveyed that the bay was his province and that he wanted to be satisfied that everybody was safe and having a good time. The salt water ran down his tanned body and began to dry off. He was covered with a very fine dust of greyish-white salt, as delicate as the pollen-dust on a nettle.

The sea was dotted with heads where people were swimming about. Here and there, little groups stood in the water; parents and two or three children, sometimes swinging the youngest child up and down by its wrists so as to duck it in and out of the water, squealing and gaining confidence. Red Rocks was a wonderful place to spend a happy day. As a resort it was surely coming into its own. Long-legged boys crawled up and down the rocks, imagining themselves in wonderful danger, and two ice-cream vans were selling fast.

Jimmy counted a hundred, quite slowly, before he even allowed himself to look out to sea in Hopper's direction. Hopper was standing in the water, exactly where he had been. When he saw Jimmy look towards him he began to swim slowly away from the shore, turning his head every few strokes to see if Jimmy was watching. Jimmy pretended not to be looking at Hopper, turning his head slightly away from him but keeping his eyes steadily on his slowly bobbing head. This was it. At any moment, Hopper's arm would go up and his cry for help would come to Jimmy across the water.

Jimmy turned once more, moving his feet and going round in a complete circle. The Life Guard's hut stood proudly at the upper edge of the beach, a sign that Red Rocks meant business and that there was enough work there for any honest young man who had no wish to go off to the city and be apprenticed and live in a hostel. As Jimmy's eyes rested on the hut, Hopper's sharp cry came suddenly to his ears. "*Help.*" It was a single, high stab of sound. If Jimmy had not been listening for it he would probably never have heard it among all the other sounds that littered the water, the laughter and the shouts of children and the insistent barking of a small dog that ran along the beach. But he did hear it, he whipped round and there was good old Hopper with his arm up, waving. None of the other bathers seemed to have noticed Hopper's distress signals, but that did not matter. He, Jimmy, the Life Guard, had noticed them. He ran forward for a few yards, then did a running dive into the water and began to swim fast, cutting past family groups and a fat pale man floating on his back in striped trunks.

Jimmy swam easily, saving his strength for the rescue, but still nearly at racing speed. He did not want Hopper to have time to get tired of pretending and let his feet down to the bottom. That would make them both look ridiculous. He kept his eyes on Hopper and presently he saw the arm go up again. Then Hopper's head disappeared, for a second or two, right under the surface. Good, he was making a real, convincing job of it. Jimmy increased his speed, taking great controlled breaths every time his mouth came clear of the water. Soon have him out of that now.

As he swam on, he realised that Hopper must be further out than he had seemed to be, from the shore. It was taking him quite some time to reach the spot. Jimmy increased his speed again, going full out now, his heart pounding with effort and excitement. For a few strokes his head was under water, and when he lifted it again he saw that he was quite close to Hopper. Then he saw the expression on Hopper's wild white face. It made his inside go cold.

Hopper's eyes were turned upward as if help might come from the sky. He did not see Jimmy close to him, but took a great struggling gasp and shouted up into the air.

"Drowning..."

Water slopped into his mouth and he coughed and went down again.

"Hopper," Jimmy called. "I'm here, I've got you."

He propelled himself forward and got hold of Hopper from behind, putting his arm round Hopper's chest so as to pull him on to his back. Then it would be easy for him to breathe as he was pulled along. But Hopper struggled like a person in a nightmare. He tried to beat Jimmy off as if Jimmy were an octopus.

Jimmy tried to call out to Hopper, to calm him, but they were fighting too fiercely. If he opened his mouth, water poured into it. So he concentrated on pulling Hopper over on his back and kicking out for the shore. He would succeed in doing this for a few minutes, and then Hopper would struggle so violently that they would get twisted into a knot and start to sink. After one of these struggles, Jimmy managed to get Hopper into the right position and begin to move him along, but after a while he sensed that there was something wrong, and lifting his head he saw that they were going the wrong way and had moved some distance further out to sea. He tried to swing Hopper round in the water, but Hopper resisted again and began to thrash wildly with his arms.

"Drowning," he said.

"I've got you," Jimmy spluttered.

Hopper went down again. Jimmy pulled him up at the cost of going under himself. When he surfaced, their faces were close together and Hopper was looking straight into his eyes. But Jimmy could not tell whether Hopper recognised him or not.

"Help me," Hopper groaned, right into Jimmy's face.

"I've got you."

They struggled and swayed in the water. Then Hopper seemed to get cramp or something. He doubled up and his head went right under again. Jimmy pulled him out and started to kick back towards the shore. Thank goodness, Hopper was quiet now. He had him in the correct grip and everything was going to be all right.

Jimmy was beginning to feel tired, but he did not slacken his efforts. There would be time to rest when they were on dry land. He kicked steadily, and held Hopper tight, and used his free arm in a backward crawl stroke. This went on for a long time, until Jimmy began to think that they must be getting in to shore. There must surely be other bathers round them. Perhaps he could call out and get a bit of help from someone. There would be nothing to be ashamed of in that, now he had brought Hopper out of danger. He lifted his head from the water, but could not see anyone close by. Still holding Hopper carefully out of the water, he twisted his body round to look towards the shore. It was no nearer. In fact the people walking about seemed like dots, and the bathing huts like dog kennels.

They were not getting any nearer to the shore. They must be in a current.

Jimmy kept calm. He had known these currents for years. This very one, he supposed, was the one he had planned to keep Hopper clear of. He had told Hopper exactly what part of the sea to go to, and Hopper had done as he said, but they were in the current all the same. That was because the currents were so unpredictable. They seemed to wander about the bay. This one was much further over than it usually came.

Hopper jerked up and down in the water. He got his face clear and gave a scream, up towards the clouds. It was as if he no longer cared about the land and had pinned all his hopes on being lifted up into the sky. He went under in mid-scream and it was obvious that his lungs had filled with water. Jimmy felt he ought to beat him on the back, but if he turned him face downwards to beat him on the back his face would be under water and his lungs would fill up faster than ever. Jimmy felt that stab of cold again. He had been afraid for some minutes, but this was different, this was panic. He wanted to shout for help himself.

Then a speckled gull came flapping slowly overhead, flying very low, examining the surface of the sea for traces of things to eat. It passed over Jimmy's head at a height of no more than three or four feet. At once Jimmy felt his panic leave him. The bird's presence seemed to domesticate the sea. Jimmy and Hopper were fighting for their lives, but to the gull this was just an ordinary afternoon and the sea was where it lived and where its food came from. The gull could at any time settle on the water and rest till it wanted to fly again. Well, so could a man. Jimmy turned over on his back and floated, taking deep breaths and holding on to Hopper's arm: Hopper thrashed about a few more times, but Jimmy held on to his arm and let him get on with it. I'm the engine of this ship, he said to himself. If I rest a minute and get my strength back, I can get us out of this.

The water felt cold, and the strength took a long time to come back to Jimmy's muscles. But his brain was clear and he used the interval to think what to do. He knew from experience that the way to get clear of one of these currents was not to swim head-on against it, as he had been trying to do, but to swim diagonally through it, aiming at the shore but only indirectly, at an angle of thirty or forty degrees. When he felt able to start again, he steered at this angle, pulling Hopper with him. But at once he noticed a change in Hopper. He was not struggling, nor even holding his body rigid. He was simply floating on the water, offering no resistance. Jimmy lifted his head up and tried to look at Hopper's face, but it was difficult from that angle. Hopper seemed to have his eyes open: was that a good sign? Had he calmed down, trusting in Jimmy and waiting for them to get back to shallow water?

The current was dragging at them; Jimmy could feel it. He stopped thinking and put every atom of his strength into swimming steadily backwards at the angle he had chosen. His arms and legs worked like small, potent machines. Now and again, when fatigue threatened to put cramp into his muscles, he altered his stroke or varied the ratio of leg-thrusts to arm-thrusts. Hours seemed to go by. He did not dare raise himself and look towards the shore in case it was no nearer, or even further off. He knew that if it was he would despair and give up. But he must keep on, not only for his own sake but for Hopper's. He even thought, briefly, of Mr Prendergast and the Development Group, who had shown confidence in him.

Hopper would never forgive him. Ten pounds would not compensate him for a fright like this. He had passed out. Jimmy slammed shut the steel door of his mind against any other thought. Hopper had fainted, he was floating peacefully. He would soon come round when they got to shore. Jimmy understood about artificial respiration and the kiss of life. All he had to do was keep going, not faint himself. The only thing that could possibly make him faint was fear, the horrible suggestion that kept leaking out like gas through the steel doors. *Has he died? Are you swimming on and on without hope, towing a lump of dead meat through the water?*

And if he has died, wouldn't it be better to let the current carry you out to sea with him, both of you lost forever, beyond recovery and beyond questioning?

Jimmy kept the steel doors shut and summoned up all the strength that remained to him. Soon he must either get to shore or be drowned. Suddenly, out of the corner of his eye, he saw a white, floating shape with a striped patch in the middle. It was the fat floating man whom he had passed on the way out, in what now seemed another life. He was lying on his back in the water as peacefully as Hopper. Jimmy reared up and looked round, letting Hopper float free for a moment. The shore was only about ten yards away, the Life Guard's hut was quite close, there were people playing and standing about in the water, he was there and nobody had noticed them struggling for their lives.

Jimmy was mistaken on this last point. In the usual patchy way in which things happen, some people had noticed that something was wrong and others had not. The fat man who was floating by himself was one of those who had not. But other people had seen Jimmy and Hopper and had called to one another and swum towards them. As Jimmy came in to the shore, they began to converge, and to call to friends on the beach, who came hurrying up. They gave instructions to each other and one tall man declared himself to be a doctor.

Jimmy bumped on the sand. They were safe. He stood up and found that the water came only to his knees. He bent over Hopper, who was floating like a wet log in the mild surf. Hopper's face was very stiff and his eyes were wide open. The salt water was washing in and out of his eyes: you would think he would have to shut them. Jimmy let go of Hopper and fell on to his hands and knees in the water and started vomiting.

Now he and Hopper were surrounded by a small crowd of people, wet swimmers and dry non-swimmers. They left Jimmy alone with his spreading patch of vomit that floated on the water, and pulled Hopper on to the sand. The doctor bent over him and everybody else stood by, jostling a little to see what was happening, but not talking much. Some children who were trying to see between the legs of the grown-ups were sent off to look for a policeman, partly because a policeman would be useful for taking statements and partly to stop them looking at Hopper.

Jimmy could hear nothing but his own retching, which was so loud that it seemed to fill the sky and press down on the sea. Between spasms he tried to tell God that he would do anything if only God would let Hopper not be dead. After a while he stopped retching and stood up. No one took any notice of him and he began to walk out of the water, past the stiff shape of Hopper and the bending and peering people. Then his way was blocked by the dark immovable bulk of the policeman.

Of course Jimmy knew the village policeman of Red Rocks, it was Mr Walker, there was nothing to be afraid of. But this was a new Mr Walker, slab-faced, hard, a taker of statements.

"I shall want your account of how this happened," he said.

"Is he – " said Jimmy. He could not say the word "dead".

"You were on duty and you saw that he was getting into difficulties?"

"I was in the sea. He called out," said Jimmy.

"Let the boy get dressed," said the doctor, looking up from where he knelt beside Hopper. "We don't want a pneumonia case on our hands as well as a death."

A death?

"Go and get dry and I'll take your statement in the hut," said policeman Walker to Jimmy.

They can't prove anything, said Jimmy inside himself as he moved away. His legs were unsteady; his knees were very loose and everything else was very tight. He thought he would never stop shivering. They can't prove that Hopper did it because I offered to pay him. The current caught him, it might have happened to anybody. It was true what they said about the current. You could just manage it if you were on your own, a strong swimmer, but not with somebody else to hold up, it hadn't been his fault.

"I did my best," he said aloud. His voice was carried away down the beach by the unnoticing wind. "Nobody could have saved him," he said loudly. "He went too far out." Then he began to cry. Tears blurred the outline of the hut as he went towards it. Fumbling for the door handle, he got safely inside. A few people who came and stood near the hut could hear him sobbing.

"He's upset, poor lad."

"No wonder he's upset. He's supposed to stop this kind of thing happening, that's what he's there for."

Agnes, who was listening among the others, said nothing.

After about ten minutes, policeman Walker came up and rapped on the door of the hut.

"Are you ready to talk now, lad?" he called through the wood.

Jimmy opened the door. He was still not dressed or even dried.

"Come on, come on, lad," said the policeman not unkindly. "Try not to go to pieces. You needn't give your evidence till later on if you don't feel up to it. Get along home and ask your mother to give you a cup of tea with a drop of whisky in it. I'll step up to the house later on."

"Is he – " Jimmy said again.

"They've done what they can for him," said the policeman. "But they haven't started him breathing and they never will now. His heart can't have been strong. There'll be a post mortem of course. If it does turn out that his heart was weak, that'll let you out of course."

"Let me out?"

"No dereliction of duty," said policeman Walker heavily. "A man with a weak heart might die any time."

I didn't know he had a weak heart, God. He didn't even know it himself. He'd have said so, wouldn't he? Then I'd never have suggested the idea. Is God angry with me? Am I wicked, a murderer? Thou shalt not kill. Tell that to the sea, God. It was the sea killed him, sucked him under. *Help me*, he said. I'll see his face every night. *Help me*.

"I tried to," he said to the place where Hopper had stood. "I tried to help you."

"Get along home now," said policeman Walker.

As Jimmy walked up the long road between the straggling houses, he met two or three families walking the other way, towards the sea. They were carrying bathing costumes and towels and the children had buckets and spades. One child had a whizzer with celluloid wings that went round and round. These people had relaxed, holiday faces. They did not know that the afternoon had been darkened. They thought the sparkling waves were still innocent.

Jimmy's house was near the T-junction of the village. He had to walk the whole length of the road before he could go to his bedroom and be out of the sound of voices and the look of eyes. He would tell his mother he was exhausted from rescuing somebody and needed to rest. That would make her leave him alone, and later, when policeman Walker came to get his statement, he could pretend to be surprised that Hopper had died. He could say he thought the doctor was with him and that he would be all right. After all, though policeman Walker had said Hopper would never breathe again, he did not *know*. The doctor was still working on Hopper and perhaps it would all come right. Oh,

God, make it come right.

Light footsteps pattered quickly after him. He turned, and it was Agnes who came running up. Jimmy stopped. There was a gap in the houses where they stood, and no one was near them.

"I s'pose you think you can just walk away," said Agnes. "Well, you can't. I know it was your fault Len got drowned."

Yes, that was Hopper's name, Len. At least that had been his name when he was alive.

"I tried to rescue him. The current's strong just there," said Jimmy.

"You killed him," said Agnes calmly.

"I – " he choked, "it was an accident."

"You gave him ten pounds to go swimming and get out of his depth."

"I never told him to get out of his depth."

"How could he pretend to be drowning if he wasn't? You killed him, Jimmy Townsend, it was you and nobody else."

"You can't prove it."

"I know where that piece of paper is. The one that says IOU."

"Why aren't you upset?" he asked her, suddenly curious about her calm blankness. "Don't you care about Hop – about Len?"

"I do care," she said. "I'm going to tell everybody that you killed him and then they'll hang you. Then that'll be fair."

"They won't hang me."

"They will when they know you killed him."

"They don't hang people any more."

"They'll lock you up in prison, Jimmy Townsend, for ever, and that's just as bad."

"It isn't," he said, thinking of the rope and the trap door.

"I'm going to take that piece of paper to Mr Walker."

"How d'you know about it, anyway?" he asked dully.

"I was listening through the door of the hut."

Little spy. She was as horrible as the most horrible side of Hopper. Jimmy glanced quickly to right and left, along the village street. There was no one about. He shot out his hand and grabbed Agnes's thin wrist. His fingers were very strong and he held the wrist in a fierce, pain-giving grip.

"Oh. Let me go. Let go of me."

"Listen," Jimmy breathed. "If you tell anybody what you heard, I'll kill you. I'll get at you and I'll kill you. You say I killed Hopper, well, if I can be a murderer once I can be one twice."

"You're hurting me – you're breaking my – "

"They won't believe you anyway. It'll only be your word against mine because that paper doesn't say what the money was for and they can't prove anything. But I'll kill you just the same, I'll kill you, I'll kill you."

Without letting go of Agnes's wrist, he moved his other hand and gripped her by the shoulder. He had her backed against the churchyard wall now, holding her by the left wrist and right shoulder, hurting her in both places. Her bones felt as small and thin as a rabbit's. Suddenly it came to him that he was enjoying squeezing her in his hands. The strength of his fingers on Agnes's light bones was a pleasure to him because she was a girl. Even to hurt her was a pleasure. To hurt a boy would have been nothing.

At the thought, he took his hands off her as if she had become electrified, and stood back. She was crying, but calmly.

"That's something else you've done," she whispered. "Cruelty to children. I'm only ten."

Jimmy looked down at his hands. They seemed to him like the hands of a murderer. How had this happened to him? His nature had changed. All summer, till this, he had been as innocent as a seagull.

He stepped backward again, putting more space between himself and Agnes, as if to let her see that he was not going to attack her.

"Listen," he said. "I didn't mean it. I won't kill you. Tell them everything, see? I won't even be angry. I don't care any more. I shan't care when they take me away from here."

He could not explain, could not find words for his need to escape from his terrible, unrecognisable new self; and she said nothing. In the silence, Jimmy could hear the swish and boom of the waves on the beach. Turning his back on the sound, he walked rapidly away towards the village. Whatever happened, he knew that he would soon be leaving.

Manhood

Swiftly free-wheeling, their breath coming easily, the man and the boy steered their bicycles down the short dip which led them from woodland into open country. Then they looked ahead and saw that the road began to climb.

"Now, Rob," said Mr Willison, settling his plump haunches firmly on the saddle, "just up that rise and we'll get off and have a good rest."

"Can't we rest now?" the boy asked. "My legs feel all funny. As if they're turning to water."

"Rest at the top," said Mr Willison firmly. "Remember what I told you? The first thing any athlete has to learn is to break the fatigue barrier."

"I've broken it already. I was feeling tired when we were going along the main road and I – "

"When fatigue sets in, the thing to do is keep going until it wears off. Then you get your second wind and your second endurance."

"I've already done that."

"Up we go," said Mr Willison, "and at the top we'll have a good rest." He panted slightly and stood on his pedals causing his machine to sway from side to side in a laboured manner. Rob, falling silent, pushed doggedly at his pedals. Slowly, the pair wavered up the straight road to the top. Once there, Mr Willison dismounted with exaggerated steadiness, laid his bicycle carefully on its side, and spread his jacket on the ground before sinking down to rest. Rob slid hastily from the saddle and flung himself full length on the grass.

"Don't lie there," said his father. "You'll catch cold."

"I'm all right. I'm warm."

"Come and sit on this. When you're overheated, that's just when you're prone to – "

"I'm all right, Dad. I want to lie here. My back aches."

"Your back needs strengthening, that's why it aches. It's a pity we don't live near a river where you could get some rowing."

The boy did not answer, and Mr Willison, aware that he was

beginning to sound like a nagging, over-anxious parent, allowed himself to be defeated and did not press the suggestion about Rob's coming to sit on his jacket. Instead, he waited a moment and then glanced at his watch.

"Twenty to twelve. We must get going in a minute."

"What? I thought we were going to have a rest."

"Well, we're having one, aren't we?" said Mr Willison reasonably. "I've got my breath back, so surely you must have."

"My back still aches. I want to lie here a bit."

"Sorry," said Mr Willison, getting up and moving over to his bicycle. "We've got at least twelve miles to do and lunch is at one."

"Dad, why did we have to come so far if we've got to get back for one o'clock? I know, let's find a telephone box and ring up Mum and tell her we –."

"Nothing doing. There's no reason why two fit men shouldn't cycle twelve miles in an hour and ten minutes."

"But we've already done about a million miles."

"We've done about fourteen, by my estimation," said Mr Willison stiffly. "What's the good of going for a bike ride if you don't cover a bit of distance?"

He picked up his bicycle and stood waiting. Rob, with his hand over his eyes, lay motionless. His legs looked thin and white among the rich grass.

"Come on, Rob."

The boy showed no sign of having heard. Mr Willison got on to his bicycle and began to ride slowly away. "Rob," he called over his shoulder, "I'm going."

Rob lay like a sullen corpse by the road side. He looked horribly like a victim of an accident, unmarked but dead from internal injuries. Mr Willison cycled fifty yards, then a hundred, then turned in a short, irritable circle and came back to where his son lay.

"Rob, is there something the matter or are you just being awkward?"

The boy removed his hand and looked up into his father's face. His eyes were surprisingly mild: there was no fire of rebellion in them.

"I'm tired and my back aches. I can't go on yet."

"Look, Rob," said Mr Willison gently, "I wasn't going to tell you this, because I meant it to be a surprise, but when you get home you'll find a present waiting for you."

"What kind of present?"

"Something special I bought for you. The man's coming this morning to fix it up. That's one reason why I suggested a bike ride this morning. He'll have it done by now."

"What is it?"

"Aha. It's a surprise. Come on, get on your bike and let's go home and see."

Rob sat up and slowly clambered to his feet. "Isn't there a short cut home?"

"I'm afraid not. It's only twelve miles."

Rob said nothing.

"And a lot of that's downhill," Mr Willison added brightly. His own legs were tired and his muscles fluttered unpleasantly. In addition, he suddenly realised he was very thirsty. Rob still without speaking picked up his bicycle and they pedalled away.

"Where is he?" Mrs Willison asked, coming into the garage.

"Gone up to his room," said Mr Willison. He doubled his fist and gave the punchball a thudding blow. "Seems to have fixed it pretty firmly. You gave him the instructions, I suppose."

"What's he doing up in his room? It's lunch-time."

"He said he wanted to rest a bit."

"I hope you're satisfied," said Mrs Willison. "A lad of thirteen, nearly fourteen years of age, just when he should have a really big appetite, and when the lunch is put on the table he's resting – "

"Now look, I know what I'm – "

"Lying down in his room, resting, too tired to eat because you've dragged him up hill and down dale on one of your – "

"We did nothing that couldn't be reasonably expected of a boy of his age."

"How do you know?" Mrs Willison demanded. "You never did anything of that kind when you were a boy. How do you know what can be reasonably – "

"Now look," said Mr Willison "When I was a boy, it was study, study, study all the time, with the fear of unemployment and insecurity in everybody's mind. I was never even given a bicycle. I never boxed, I never rowed, I never did anything to develop my physique. It was just work, work, work, pass this exam, get that certificate. Well, I did it and now I'm qualified and in a secure job. But you know as well as I do that they let me down. Nobody encouraged me to build myself up."

"Well what does it matter? You're all right – "

"Grace!" Mr Willison interrupted sharply. I am not all right and you know it. I am under average height, my chest is flat and I'm – "

"What nonsense. You're taller than I am and I'm – "

"No son of mine is going to grow up with the same wretched physical heritage that I – "

"No, he'll just have heart disease through overtaxing his strength, because you haven't got the common sense to – "

"His heart is one hundred per cent all right. Not three weeks have gone by since the doctor looked at him."

"Well why does he get so overtired if he's all right? Why is he lying down now instead of coming to the table, a boy of his age?"

A slender shadow blocked part of the dazzling sun in the doorway. Looking up simultaneously, the Willisons greeted their son.

"Lunch ready, Mum? I'm hungry."

"Ready when you are," Grace Willison beamed. "Just wash your hands and come to the table."

"Look Rob," said Mr Willison. "If you hit it with your left hand and then catch it on the rebound with your right it's excellent ring training." He dealt the punchball two amateurish blows. "That's what they call a right cross," he said.

"I think it's fine. I'll have some fun with it," said Rob. He watched mildly as his father peeled off the padded mittens.

"Here, slip these on," said Mr Willison. "They're just training gloves. They harden your fists. Of course, we can get a pair of proper gloves later. But these are specially for use with the ball."

"Lunch," called Mrs Willison from the house.

"Take a punch at it," Mr Willison urged.

"Let's go and eat."

"Go on. One punch before you go in. I haven't seen you hit it yet."

Rob took the gloves, put on the righthand one, and gave the punchball one conscientious blow, aiming at the exact centre.

"Now let's go in," he said.

"Lunch!"

"All right. We're coming..."

"Five feet eight, Rob," said Mr Willison, folding up the wooden ruler. "You're taller than I am. This is a great landmark."

"Only just taller."

"But you're growing all the time. Now all you have to do is to start growing outwards as well as upwards. We'll have you in the middle of that scrum. The heaviest forward in the pack."

Rob picked up his shirt and began uncertainly poking his arms into his sleeves.

"When do they pick the team?" Mr Willison asked. "I should have thought they'd have done it by now."

"They have done it," said Rob. He bent down to pick up his socks from under a chair.

"They have? And you – "

"I wasn't selected," said the boy, looking intently at the socks as if trying to detect minute differences in colour and weave.

Mr Willison opened his mouth, closed it again, and stood for a minute looking out of the window. Then he gently laid his hand on his son's shoulder. "Bad luck," he said quietly.

"I tried hard," said Rob quickly.

"I'm sure you did."

"I played my hardest in the trial games."

"It's just bad luck," said Mr Willison. "It could happen to anybody."

There was silence as they both continued with their dressing. A faint smell of frying rose into the air, and they could hear Mrs Willison laying the table for breakfast.

"That's it, then, for this season," said Mr Willison, as if to himself.

"I forgot to tell you, though," said Rob. "I was selected for the boxing team."

"You were? I didn't know the school had one."

"It's new. Just formed. They had some trials for it at the end of last term. I found my punching was better than most people's because I'd been getting plenty of practice with the ball.

Mr Willison put out a hand and felt Rob's biceps. "Not bad, not bad at all," he said critically. "But if you're going to be a boxer and represent the school, you'll need more power up there I tell you what. We'll train together."

"That'll be fun," said Rob. "I'm training at school too."

"What weight do they put you in?"

"It isn't weight, it's age. Under fifteen. Then when you get over fifteen you get classified into weights."

"Well," said Mr Willison, tying his tie, "you'll be in a good position for the under-fifteens. You've got six months to play with. And there's no reason why you shouldn't steadily put muscle on all the time. I suppose you'll be entered as a team, for tournaments and things?"

"Yes. There's a big one at the end of next term. I'll be in that."

Confident, joking, they went down to breakfast. "Two eggs for Rob, Mum," said Mr Willison. "He's in training. He's going to be a heavyweight."

"A heavyweight what?" Mrs Willison asked, teapot in hand.

"Boxer," Rob smiled.

Grace Willison put down the teapot, her lips compressed and looked from one to the other. "Boxing?" she repeated.

"Boxing," Mr Willison replied calmly.

"Over my dead body", said Mrs Willison. "That's one sport I'm definite that he's never going in for."

"Too late. They've already picked him for the under-fifteens. He's had trials and everything."

"Is this true Rob?" she demanded.

"Yes," said the boy, eating rapidly.

"Well, you can just tell them you're dropping it. Baroness Summerskill – "

"To hell with Baroness Summerskill!" her husband shouted. "The first time he gets a chance to do something, the first time he gets picked for a team and given a chance to show what he's made of, and you have to bring up Baroness Summerskill."

"But it injures their brains! All those blows on the front of the skull. I've read about it – "

"Injures their brains!" Mr Willison snorted. "Has it injured Muhammad Ali's brain? Why, he's one of the acutest business men in the world!"

"Rob," said Mrs Willison steadily, "when you get to school, go and see the sports master and tell him you're giving up boxing."

"There isn't a sports master. All the masters do bits of it at different times."

"There must be one who's in charge of the boxing. All you have to do is tell him – "

"Are you ready Rob?" said Mr Willison. "You'll be late for school if you don't go."

"I'm in plenty of time, Dad. I haven't finished my breakfast."

"Never mind, push along, old son. You've had your egg and bacon, that's what matters. I want to talk to your mother."

Mrs Willison did not lift her eyes from the television set as her husband entered. "All ready now, Mother." said Mr Willison.

"He's going to rest in bed now, and go along at about six o'clock. I'll go with him and wait till the doors open to be sure of a ring-side seat." He sat down on the sofa beside his wife and tried to put his arm around her. "Come on love," he said coaxingly. "Don't spoil my big night."

She turned to him and he was startled to see her eyes brimming with angry tears. "What about my big night?" she asked, her voice harsh. "Fourteen years ago, remember? When he came into the world."

"Well, what about it?" Mr Willison parried, uneasily aware that the television set was quacking and signalling on the fringe of his attention, turning the scene from clumsy tragedy into clumsier farce.

"Why didn't you tell me then?" she sobbed. "Why did you let me have a son if all you were interested in was having him punched to death by a lot of rough bullet-headed louts who – "

"Take a grip on yourself Grace. A punch on the nose won't hurt him."

"You're an unnatural father," she keened. "I don't know how you can bear to send him into that ring to be beaten and thumped – Oh, why can't you stop him now? Keep him at home? There's no law that compels us to – "

"That's where you're wrong Grace," said Mr Willison sternly. "There is a law. The unalterable law of nature that says that the young males of the species indulge in manly trials of strength. Think of all the other lads who are going into the ring tonight. D'you think their mothers are sitting about crying and kicking up a fuss? No – they're proud to have strong, masculine sons who can stand up in the ring and take a few punches."

"Go away, please," said Mrs Willison, sinking back with closed eyes. "Just go right away and don't come near me until it's all over."

"Grace!"

"Please, please leave me alone. I can't bear to look at you and I can't bear to hear you."

"You're hysterical," said Mr Willison bitterly. Rising, he went out into the hall and called up the stairs. "Are you in bed, Rob?"

There was a slight pause and then Rob's voice called faintly "Could you come up, Dad?"

"Come up? Why? Is there something the matter?"

"Could you come up?"

Mr Willison ran up the stairs. "What is it?" he panted. "D'you want something?"

"I think I've got appendicitis," said Rob. He lay squinting among the pillows, his face suddenly narrow and crafty.

"I don't believe you," said Mr Willison shortly. "I've supervised your training for fifteen weeks and I know you're as fit as a fiddle. You can't possibly have anything wrong with you."

"I've got a terrible pain in my side," said Rob. "Low down on the righthand side. That's where appendicitis comes, isn't it?"

Mr Willison sat down on the bed. "Listen Rob," he said. "Don't do this to me. All I'm asking you to do is to go into the ring and have one bout. You've been picked for the school team and everyone's depending on you."

"I'll die if you don't get the doctor," Rob suddenly hissed. "Mum!" he shouted.

Mrs Willison came bounding up the stairs. "What is it, my pet?"

"My stomach hurts. Low down on the right hand side."

"Appendicitis!" she whirled to face Mr Willison. "That's what comes of your foolishness!"

"I don't believe it," said Mr Willison. He went out of the bedroom and down the stairs.

The television was still jabbering in the living room, and for fifteen minutes Mr Willison forced himself to sit staring at the strident puppets, glistening in metallic light, as they enacted their Lilliputian rituals. Then he went up to the bedroom again. Mrs Willison was bathing Rob's forehead.

"His temperature's normal," she said.

"Of course his temperature's normal," said Mr Willison. "He doesn't want to fight, that's all."

"Fetch the doctor," said a voice from under the cold flannel that swathed Rob's face.

"We will, pet, if you don't get better very soon," said Mrs Willison, darting a murderous glance at her husband.

Mr Willison slowly went down stairs. For a moment he stood looking at the telephone, then picked it up and dialled the number of the grammar school. No one answered. He replaced the receiver, went to the foot of the stairs and called, "What's the name of the master in charge of the tournament?"

"I don't know," Rob called weakly.

"You told me you'd been training with Mr Granger," Mr Willison called. "Would he know anything about it?"

Rob did not answer, so Mr Willison looked up all the Grangers in the telephone book. There were four in the town, but only one was M.A. "That's him," said Mr Willison. With lead in his heart and ice in his fingers, he dialled the number.

Mrs Granger fetched Mr Granger. Yes, he taught at the school. He was the right man. What could he do for Mr Willison?

"It's about tonight's boxing tournament."

"Sorry, what? The line's bad."

"Tonight's boxing tournament."

"Have you got the right person?"

"You teach my son Rob – we've just agreed on that. Well, it's about the boxing tournament he's supposed to be taking part in tonight."

"Where?"

"Where? At the school, of course. He's representing the under-fifteens."

There was a pause. "I'm not quite sure what mistake you're making, Mr Willison, but I think you've got hold of the wrong end of at least one stick." A hearty defensive laugh. "If Rob belongs to a boxing club it's certainly news to me, but in any case it can't be anything to do with the school. We don't go in for boxing."

"Don't go in for it?"

"We don't offer it. It's not in our curriculum."

"Oh," said Mr Willison. "Oh. Thank you. I must have – well, thank you."

"Not at all. I'm glad to answer any queries. Everything's all right I trust?"

"Oh, yes," said Mr Willison, "yes, thanks. Everything's all right."

He put down the telephone, hesitated, then turned and began slowly to climb the stairs.

King Caliban

Of course, the short explanation is that Fred's always been a bit on the daft side. That's what I said to them straight away, as soon as they began to question me. I'm his brother, I said, and you can take it from me he's never been overburdened with grey matter. I remember that those were the exact words I used. Overburdened with grey matter. Nobody could say Fred was that. But gentle, of course, with all his strength. That's why the whole thing's so ridiculous.

I don't blame them for getting me down there. Just routine. They have to make enquiries. When all's said and done, I was there and saw it happen. So did a thousand other people, of course. But they could hardly have all that lot in. And I was the one he kept talking about. "You ask Bert," he kept saying to them. "Bert'll tell you I didn't mean to do it." That's what they told me, and I can quite believe it. He always did refer things to me. I used to do the talking for him, even when we were kids, though I was eighteen months younger. Anything Fred couldn't quite explain, send for Bert. I had the brains and he had the brawn. It could have been a good partnership. I say "could have been", because as things were it never really worked out. If I'd been a type to get into scrapes, to turn people against me and find myself in a position where I needed a big strong brother to stand by me, I'd have found it very convenient to have a giant in the family. But then I wasn't. I always got along all right. I soon learnt to handle people. All you have to do is watch them – keep your eyes open. And I never got into trouble, much, either at school or when I started work. Not real trouble. A bit of boyish high spirits, yes, but to do anything really silly was never in my line. So I just never got into any trouble that I needed pulling out of.

Come to think of it, my quick wits were no more use to him, really, than his strength and size were to me. I mean to say, I could tell him this and that and the other thing, but I couldn't stop him being stupid. He was slow and that was all there was to it. Of course I always did what I could to help him. Even after we went different ways, or rather I went ahead and he stayed pretty well where he was. For quite long spells we wouldn't see much of each other. But when we did meet, I'd always ask him how he was getting on, and I was always ready to give him a hand where I could. Must do something for Fred, I used to say. Ask anybody. Well, that's how the whole thing came about, isn't it? Me helping him. That's what I said to the police. You try to help somebody, I said, and this is where you land up. In the police station, being questioned.

If he'd had just a bit more grey matter, none of this would have happened. He'd have got a decent job and earned a decent wage, and then Doreen wouldn't have got on to him so much. Another three quid a week would have satisfied her. It's as simple as that.

All right, I realise you don't know what I'm talking about. Doreen's Fred's wife. They started going together when he first went to work at Greenall's, and they got married quite soon. She was about twenty-nine when he first met her. She was pretty well in charge of the shop. Old Greenall used to call her his right-hand man. Of course she was very wide awake. Knew exactly what they had in stock, whether it was on the shelves or in store, and carried all the prices in her head. Greenall offered to put up her wages, when she said she was leaving. If what I heard at the time was anything to go by, he pretty near offered her double. Said he couldn't do without her. But she just said she'd decided to marry Fred and make a home for him, and she was leaving and that was that. She told him if he could afford to spend that much on wages he could give Fred a bit more, now that he was going to be a breadwinner. But that wouldn't wash, of course. Fred was getting seven pounds already and he wasn't worth more than that of anybody's money.

He was slow, you see. Old Greenall used to say he did a lot of work in a lot of time, and it's true that Fred was never lazy. But he couldn't hold much in his head, he had to keep coming back for instructions, and he could never see for himself the shortest way to do a thing. Greenall used to say that he kept him on because he was as strong as three men and as honest as daylight. And it's true there was a lot of heavy work about the place. There always is, with the grocery. You'd be surprised. Barrels of this and crates of that to be humped about. And loading and un-loading the van. Fred used to spend most of his time carrying things about, or doing the deliveries. He hadn't enough grey matter to do any of the paper work, and when they put him on to serving in the shop he was more of a nuisance than anything else, with being so big. The space behind the counter just wasn't wide enough for him. And as for squeezing past him to get at anything, you might as well squeeze past an elephant.

It got on Doreen's nerves from the start. I think she was fond of him in her own way, but between you and me I don't think she'd really thought out all the angles before jumping into holy wedlock. She was pretty scared of being left on the shelf – it's a thought that must come pretty often to a girl who works in a grocery store. She knew what happened when you made a mistake and over-ordered a particular line. You sold what you could, and the rest you got rid of dirt cheap, or, in the end, just chucked it away. That wasn't going to be her. Not little Doreen. As soon as she saw the magic number 30 coming up on the clock, she jumped. And she landed on Fred.

I thought he was rather lucky, at that. She wasn't a bad looker, and she was smart. But she did get on to him about money. She'd saved a bit, and by putting that to what Fred had, they managed to get a house in a decent enough street. But that was just it. They were out of Fred's class, really. Most of the husbands were getting twice what he was getting. So their wives had all sorts of things that Doreen couldn't afford. They managed a telly, but when it came to fridges and cars and stainless steel sinks, and one woman even had a washing-machine! I think it was the washing-machine that put the iron in Doreen's soul. Yes, old Fred wouldn't be in the mess he's in today if it hadn't been for the washing-machine.

One Sunday when I was round there, she really poured out her troubles to me while Fred was out in the garden. The children were with him, skipping round him as he worked and playing some kind of game. They had two, a boy and a girl. They usually stuck with Fred most of the time, when he was home. It always seemed to me that he was fonder of them than she was. Of course in a way I don't blame her. She used to work part time, until they came, so that they weren't so pinched for money. But with two kids to look after, she'd had to give it up. So she had no reason to thank them for coming into the world. Not that she didn't do her best to bring them up right.

Anyway, this Sunday afternoon she stood staring through the window at the three of them. Her face had gone into hard lines and she looked old and miserable. And when she suddenly turned to me, I knew it was coming.

"Bert," she says, jumping straight in without any messing about, "can't *you* suggest something?"

"Suggest what kind of something?" I asked.

She looked through the window at Fred and the kids. He was digging trenches, shoving the spade through the wet soil with his great arms as if it was sawdust he was shifting. I never saw anybody as strong as he was. The kids were hanging on to him, shouting something and laughing. I could hear their voices faintly, through the glass.

"What use is he?" said Doreen, following my eyes. "Tell me that. Here I am, with two kids to bring up and everything to pay for, and what does Fred do?"

"He works," I said. "He earns a living, as well as he's able."

She looked at me, straight in the eyes. "That's not well enough," she said. "You know it and I know it. We all know he's strong, but what's the good of that?"

I looked out at Fred again. He was getting on towards thirty. His body seemed all chest and shoulders. Whether his legs really were very short I don't know, but his great barrel of a torso made them seem like an ape's legs. His hair was beginning to get thin in front. As I watched, he laughed at something one of the children said, and his whole face seemed to go into one enormous smile.

"You be satisfied, that's my advice," I said to Doreen. "They don't come any better than old Fred. You'll never be rich, but you've got a good husband and the kids have got a good father."

"Keep your advice," she said, "if that's the best you can do. Mr Know-it-all. How would you like to live on seven quid, with two children? Scraping for every penny and never having a bit of life. If I want an evening out, the only thing I can afford is to go down to the station and watch the trains come in. He's your brother, and it's not good enough. Who can I turn to, if not you? You've got all the brains, you could easily think of an opening for him. Don't you tell me to be satisfied." And a lot more like that. Till she got so unpleasant I put my coat on and left.

I tried to forget about Doreen and her troubles. After all, I wasn't her brother, I was Fred's, and he seemed all right. He was quite happy. She nagged him, of course, but what I say is, if you don't want to get nagged, don't get married.

But I couldn't forget her face. She'd suddenly put on twenty years. I mean, she was desperate. And however much I tried to blink it, I had to admit that seven quid was seven quid, for a woman who'd been in a good job and never really gone short. Well, she knew Fred wasn't overburdened with grey matter, I thought to myself. It's her own fault. But that never really works. If you feel sorry for somebody, you can't stop it just by saying it's their own fault. It nags at you. In fact, if you can believe me, it really began to spoil the fun I was getting out of my own life. I was doing pretty well. I'm in building supply, you know. I had a nice little corner in porcelain stuff just then, everything from insulators to wash-basins. I was doing all right, and I'd begun to knock about with a crowd who'd mostly got a fair amount of cash. Chaps who knew their way round. I was on the inside, after always having been on the outside before, and it tasted good. I'd stopped going to the Lord Nelson in the evenings, and taken to looking in at the back bar of the George—the Private Bar. A very nice crowd used to get in there.

Anyway, the reason I mention it is because Len Weatherhead used to go there very often. He was really one of the big boys. Savile Row suits, a Bentley, the lot. He'd made it up from the ground and he wasn't fifty yet. Started as some kind of fair-ground attendant, then ran a boxing-booth, and now one of the biggest all-in wrestling promotors in the country...all-in wrestling! Can't you see how the whole thing seemed to fall smack into my lap?

And yet, funnily enough, I didn't think of it for a week or two. It wasn't until one evening when Len Weatherhead came in looking really brassed off. Dead cheesed. The corners of his mouth were right down and he wasn't speaking to anybody.

Anyway, I generally manage to open people up, and I went to work on him. Pretty soon I had him telling me what was wrong. He couldn't find wrestlers. He'd got the crowds, he'd got the halls, but he couldn't find the boys to wrestle.

"Only today," he said. "One of my best pairs. Two boys I could really rely on. Go anywhere, and always put on a good show. Mike the Moose and Billy Crusher, those were their wrestling names. Always put 'em together. Well, all of a sudden Ogden, that's Mike the Moose, comes to me and says he's dissolving the partnership and going to work somewhere as a gym instructor. Says he knows it'll mean a drop in the money, but he prefers the type of work he'll be doing. I ask you! Turning away eighty quid a week!"

"Eighty quid a *week*?" I said. All of a sudden I saw Doreen running to the shop to buy six washing-machines, one for each room.

He nodded. "In the season," he said. "Of course there's not a lot doing between April and September. But those two were a top pair. Always up near the head of the billing. And so well drilled, and accustomed to one another! Knew every wrinkle in the game. Never hurt one another, never had to have any time off with sprains or dislocations or anything like that. And the money I spent on them!"

I began to question him, without letting on that I had anything in my mind except to have an interesting conversation. I learnt a lot in a few minutes. All-in wrestling was something I'd never given any thought to, and I hadn't any idea how it was run. I suppose I just thought it was a matter of a promoter hiring a hall, and then a lot of chaps being entered by their managers, like boxers. But of course all-in isn't a contest, it's a gymnastic display. The wrestlers have to be chaps who know each other and work together. Every fight is rehearsed from beginning to end. You'll notice, if you ever watch a contest, that every time one chap has got the other down and he's putting some fearful lock on him, twisting his limbs about and making him yell blue murder, and you decide he's a goner, the one who's on top suddenly releases his hold and lets him get up. That's because it's his turn to be put through the mill next, till the crowd get tired of it and one of them has to win and make room for another pair.

You'll probably want to ask me what I asked Len Weatherhead. What kind of people watch this? How can they enjoy being treated to this kind of thing, when a child of five could see the fights were rigged? Surely it can't fool them, and if it doesn't fool them, what are they doing there? Len Weatherhead couldn't really answer this and neither can I. In a way, all that happens is that the sight of two big hefty men beating and gouging hell out of one another excites the crowd so much that they don't care whether they're being fooled or not. They don't cool down long enough to be able to think about it one way or the other. They're like middle-aged men watching a strip-tease. Every one of them knows that the girl isn't taking her clothes off for him, but never mind, he still wants to see her do it.

Len went on to tell me a bit more about how they do it. In some cases, the wrestlers have what you might call characters. The good guy against the bad guy, like Westerns. One of them will wear some costume that makes him look devilish, and have some frightening name like Chang the Terrible or Doctor Death.

He'll be fighting some blue-eyed, fair-haired upstanding type, and he'll fight dirty and put the crowd against him. Then they'll scream all sorts of insults at him, and he'll snarl at them and shake his fist, and of course the other chap will let him win right up to the end, and suddenly get the upper hand in the last half-minute and damn near break his neck. That's when they all jump up and down and shout with joy. Look at it this way, where else could they get that amount of fun for half a crown? Football's good value of course, but in football you can't guarantee that the team you support is going to win, and you don't have the fun of seeing the opposing team get kicked and trampled on. That's where all-in definitely scores. It works on some of these feeble-minded types so much that after a season or two of following it, they get to a stage where it's the only sport they *can* follow. Oh yes, somebody had a bright idea there.

"Look here, Len," I said, choosing a moment when nobody else was likely to come breezing over and listen in. Of course you know what's coming. "You're really short of wrestlers?" I asked him. "I mean, if you found a chap who was willing to go in at the bottom of the ladder and who was strong, I mean *really* strong, you'd take him on even if he had no experience?"

He looked a bit crafty at me. "It would depend," he said. "If he had no experience, I'd have to find him a suitable partner and have him trained from the ground up. And he wouldn't be making me a penny during that time. I couldn't afford to keep him on more than part-time, till he was trained."

We dickered about it a bit and finally he asked me point-blank to come out with whatever it was I had in my mind. So I told him about Fred. A man with the strength of half a dozen wrestlers rolled into one, not making a penny out of it.

Anyway, under his craftiness Len Weatherhead was as keen to do business as I was, and before we drank up and cleared out at closing time I had a nice little deal all buttoned up for Fred. He was to go down to the gym evenings and weekends, and train with this chap Billy Crusher, who'd been left without a partner. As soon as the training had reached a stage where they could work out a fight and get it rehearsed, they could go on. And when they went on, Fred would move straight into the big money. If he fought three times a week, he'd clear anything from fifty to eighty quid, depending on the gate money.

Of course Len Weatherhead said he'd have to look Fred over first, to see if what I said about him was true, but I knew that wouldn't hold us up. So far from exaggerating about his size and strength, I'd even played it down. I didn't want Len to think of me as a big-mouth. He was a man I could do a lot of business with, if I kept my eyes open and won his confidence. He clapped me on the shoulder before driving off in his Bentley and I felt on top of the world.

Well, there was no point in messing about, so the very next evening I took Fred out for a drink and started to feed the idea into his mind.

"How are the kids, Fred?" I asked him.

"They're coming along fine," he said. "I don't know which of them's growing faster. Sometimes I think it's Peter and other times I think it's Paula. They just grow and grow. And *clever*! They get it from their mother, you know. You know what they said the other day?" And he went on to tell me all their clever little sayings. I let him chatter on because I could see it was softening him up. He was doing all the work for me, and all I had to do was listen and buy him a drink now and then.

So I listened until he'd told me everything the kids had done and said since they were one day old, all of which I'd heard before because he never talked about anything else. And when he'd finished I gave the ball another tap to keep it rolling. Money.

"You've got two grand kids," I said. "Kids who deserve the best. And there are so many opportunities opening out for youngsters these days. That's where a bit of money comes in handy."

"That's what Doreen says," he said, and a look of unhappiness and worry came over his face. Fred's expression never changed quickly, like anyone else's; it seemed to take time for one to fade and another to take its place. Like sand castles being washed out by the tide. I suppose that was the slowness of his mind.

I knew there was no prospect of rushing him too fast, what with the time it took him to get hold of an idea, so I decided to jump straight in. I asked him if he'd ever heard of Len Weatherhead. He hadn't. I told him Len Weatherhead made a lot of money, for himself and everybody else, by promoting all-in wrestling. Fred thought for a bit and I half expected him to ask me what all-in wrestling was, but finally he must have decided that he'd heard of it, so he turned his head slowly towards me and said, "Yes?"

"Yes," I said. "And what's more, Len Weatherhead is very interested in you, Fred. Very interested indeed."

"Interested in me?" he said, tapping himself on the chest to make quite sure we had our identities sorted out.

"Yes, you," I said. "He's heard all about you as a big strong muscle-man. That's the main thing, you know, in the wrestling game. The rest can be learnt. They have a gym where they train you."

It was as plain as a pikestaff that he simply didn't know what I was getting at. All-in wrestling, and gym, and training just weren't anything to do with him; that was that. I felt irritated suddenly. I wanted to drag him along. Cut through that slowness of his.

"Listen, Fred," I said. "Why do you think I'm bothering to tell you this?"

"Is it a bother?" he said. "I thought we were just having a pint together."

"Well, so we are," I said. After all he was my brother. "But you're lucky, Fred. You've got a smart brother who keeps his eyes open for you."

"Well, thanks," he said.

"I can put you in the money," I said, rushing it along. "No more trouble with Doreen. Everything you want for the kids. Dress them up lovely. Take them on holidays. Send them to a nice school."

"You can do this?" he asked, looking at me with his eyes wide open. I knew I'd hit the right note.

"Just play along with me," I said, clapping him on the shoulder, "and I can put you in a position to make eighty quid a week."

At that, he burst out laughing. Or rather, laughter slowly welled up out of that big chest of his. It took about two minutes to get from his belly as far as his voice.

"All right, laugh," I said. "But when you've finished laughing, let me put you in the picture. Eighty quid sounds a lot to you. It even sounds a lot to me. But it's just everyday stuff to Len Weatherhead."

Fred searched in his memory for the name Len Weatherhead, which he'd heard about two minutes before, and finally he lifted his head in that perplexed way of his, looked at me and said: "Wrestling?"

"Wrestling," I said. "Just the job you were cut out for."

He picked up his beer as if he was going to take a swig at it, but he only looked at it and then put it down and faced me again.

"You're joking, Bert," he said. "It's one of your jokes."

"Eighty quid a week," I said. "Don't believe me. Don't listen to me. Go and see Len Weatherhead."

He shook his head.

"Now look, Fred," I said. "Do you want to have nice things for Peter and Paula or don't you?"

"They're all right," he said, almost fiercely. "They don't go short. I take care of them and we have good times together. They've got a house to live in and a garden – "

"And they could have so much more," I cut in quickly, "if their father would just realise his own potentialities.

That last word threw him, naturally. It was the sort of word you hear chucked about in the Private Bar in the George, but not in the Lord Nelson, where we were.

"Don't mess me about. Bert," he said. "Don't mess me about with long words. I do a job and the wage comes in and we live on it. We can be happy."

I didn't want to get stuck on that point, so I just pushed along. First I drew a picture of Doreen's sufferings, then I looked forward to the time when the kids were teen-agers and needed all sorts of things to help them keep up with the crowd – smart clothes and motor-scooters and the rest of it. I told him it wouldn't always be enough for them to play with him in the garden.

"You're doing all right," I said, "*now*. But wait till they get bigger. You'll need four, five times the money you're making now. Who's going to give it to you? Greenall? That's a laugh and you know it."

I got him so worried that finally he agreed to come with me and see Len Weatherhead. But first I thought I'd better take him to a wrestling bout, to give him an idea of what he was going into. I didn't want Len Weatherhead to write him off as a total nitwit the first time he met him. He had to be in the picture somewhere.

So a couple of nights later we went down to the Town Hall for one of Len's promotions. It was the usual thing – tickets from about half a crown to a quid, the place pretty well packed out, and everybody excited at the prospect of seeing some licensed mayhem.

Right from the start I knew I was going to have trouble with Fred. I'd taken a lot of trouble to get him into a nice relaxed mood, so much trouble that I really wondered, now and then, why I was doing it. Just brotherly love, was all I could think of. I'd called at his house and picked him up by car – with Doreen's

full approval, of course, because I'd told her what I was doing –
and on the way down I'd stopped and got a couple of drinks inside
him and even stood him a cigar, one of those one-and-ninepenny
Panatellas that people like Fred associate with Christmas.

But it was no good. Even before the first pair of wrestlers came
out, I could see that he didn't like it. The atmosphere upset him.
There was a kind of edge to it that upset him. Of course he was
always so gentle, he hated any kind of upset or violence. As we sat
there waiting, I looked round at the scene and for a moment I saw
it through his eyes. There was the huge hall, dimly lit, with clouds
of cigarette-smoke drifting up to the ceiling. And the ring, with all
that white light beating down on it, like an operating table all
ready for someone's guts to be cut out. And the faces of the people
sitting round us weren't too pleasant, some of them. Probably you
wouldn't have minded them in a crowd, but here they seemed
more ugly and cruel, with the sort of thoughts that were going on
in their minds.

Then I thought, *eighty quid a week!* And I knew I'd talk Fred
into it, with Doreen's help, whatever he thought about this
evening.

Well, it started, and I must say I hardly saw anything of the
programme. I was too busy hanging on to Fred, trying to calm
him down and make him stay in his seat. If I hadn't been there I
don't think he'd have stayed beyond the first minute of the first
bout. There was all the usual razzmatazz, the M.C. coming out
and shouting the names, and then the ref. and the two fighters
going into a huddle. One called Eskimo Jim was the bad one. You
could see at once he was going to fight dirty. He didn't look much
like a real Eskimo, but he had thick lips and a flat nose and his
eyes were sort of slanted. The Irish chap was good-looking, of
course. It was the most obvious bit of pairing-off you could
imagine. All the time the ref. was briefing them, or pretending to,
the crowd were barracking Eskimo Jim and he was glaring murder at them, but the ref. pulled him back, of course. And all the
time Paddy stood looking calm and handsome. I'd have laughed
if I hadn't been so worried about the way Fred was taking it. He
didn't seem to see the funny side at all. The insults and the
shouting, and the fist-shaking and threats, were all having a
terrible effect on him. It was like trying to lead a horse past
something it's afraid of. "Relax, Fred, relax," I kept saying to
him. "It's just entertainment, see? It's not a fight – it's an acrobatic performance. Remember that – just an acrobatic perform-

ance." And just as I said the words, Eskimo Jim pushed the referee to one side and started to fight before Paddy was ready. Of course. He jumped at him, grabbed his head, and swung it down to knee-level, twisting it at the same time so that he damn near dragged it off. Then, while Paddy was reeling about all dazed, he gave him a kick in the guts that you could hear all over the building. It was very clever, really, the way they managed it. But it was too much for Fred. He was out of his seat in an instant, and if we hadn't been sitting in the middle of a row he'd have been half-way down the aisle and I'd never have got him back. It was the other customers who saved the situation for me. They'd paid for their seats, the butchery had only just begun and they didn't want their view blocked right away by this big elk of a man pushing past them. They turned and hissed at him to sit down, and he did. But he wouldn't look at the ring.

Well, we stuck it out. About half-way through the evening, Fred seemed to slump in his seat, as if the will to resist had left him, and he didn't try to get away anymore. Just sat there staring straight in front of him. I couldn't even decide, when I glanced at him, whether he was watching the wrestlers or not. As for me, I settled down and watched the show. After all, I'd paid for it. And if Fred wasn't concentrating, then I'd got to watch hard enough for two. I don't like to waste my money.

We went across to the pub afterwards and I lined up a couple of refreshing pints. Fred threw his down in about four swallows. I could see his hand trembling as he lifted the glass. There was no need to ask him what he thought about all-in wrestling.

"Well, that's it, Fred," I said. "I'm not going to try to talk you into anything. I've lined up a chance for you, and if you don't want to take it, that's your affair."

He turned and looked at me. His face was dead white: I'd never seen it like that before. "You mean you still want me to go in for *that*?" he asked. I didn't answer, and he didn't say anything more. I finished my pint and then I drove him home. Well, I was thinking to myself, that's one more thing that's no good.

Doreen was waiting for us when we got back to the house. I was feeling pretty savage about wasting all that time and money, and when she asked me to come in for a cup of tea, I said *no*. In fact I didn't even get out of the car. She called to me from the doorway and when she saw I wasn't going to move, she came to the gate and spoke to me through the car window.

"What's wrong?" she asked in her direct way.

"Oh, nothing," I said. "Fred doesn't like all-in wrestling, that's all. We'll have to think of some other spare-time hobby for him."

And I drove off. Let him sort it out, I thought. I could imagine him trying to explain to Doreen that he didn't want to go in for wrestling even if it did mean eighty quid a week. And, being in a savage mood, I felt it served him right. I'd had a lot of trouble and expense, and what was worse, I was going to look a big-mouth when I next talked to Len Weatherhead. Just a stupid, unreliable big-mouth. Let her put him through it, I thought as I locked up the garage.

After that, I just assumed it was all over. I kept away from the George for the next few evenings, because I wouldn't have known what to say to Len Weatherhead if I'd met him. I thought I'd let the idea just get lost of its own accord. Anyway, it was a good thing I didn't rush into any big explanation with Len, because the next thing that happened was something that really surprised me.

I was sitting in the office one morning. I call it the office, though it's only one room and I still do all my own secretarial work. But that won't last. I've got my eye on a bigger place already, and business is looking up all the time. Anyway, I was sitting there, working out a bit of costing on some wash-hand basins, when the door opened – there was Fred. In the middle of the morning, I ask you.

"What's up?" I said. "Got the sack?"

"I'm on deliveries," he said. "I just wanted to look in and have a word with you."

"What about?" I said. Rather cool. I wasn't in a mood to let him forget that he'd disappointed me.

"Look," he said, coming all the way into the room, but not sitting down. "This Len Who's it. When can you take me to him?"

I looked up into his face and all of a sudden I saw what must have happened. He looked like somebody who'd just been repatriated from Devil's Island.

"Been talking things over with Doreen, have you?" I asked him, keeping it as casual as I could.

"When can I see this Len?" he asked, ignoring my question. Of course he wouldn't want to talk about it. Doreen must have really turned it loose on him, to drive him to the state where he'd rather go into the ring with Eskimo Jim than face her in his own house.

I reached for the telephone and dialled Len Weatherhead's office number. I wasn't going to let this go cool. Too much depended on it. The luck was with me: he was in and I got hold of him straight away. Before I hung up I had it all fixed for Fred to go and see him and talk business.

After that, I relaxed. I knew that Fred wouldn't change his mind. He might change his mind about wanting to be a wrestler, but he wouldn't go back on his arrangement to see Len Weatherhead. Which made it Weatherhead's job to talk him into it. All I had to do was to sit back and collect thanks and smiles all round.

The next few days passed very smoothly. I largely by-passed Fred and got the score from Doreen. She welcomed me, now, as nice as pie. I was the life-saver who had turned her grocer's-assistant husband into a big, rich wrestler. At least he was headed that way. Len had evidently taken to him and seen how far his strength would take him in the wrestling business, because he'd given him the full treatment. Taken him all round the gym and everything. If Fred still wanted to back out, he didn't get a chance to, because the next thing Len did was to arrange for him to meet Billy Crusher. That's the fellow who was in partnership with Mike the Moose, who'd now gone legit. as a gym instructor.

I suppose Billy did more than anyone to talk Fred into the game. He had a professional attitude, which was all the more refreshing because he was going to be with Fred, right there in the ring. He wasn't asking Fred to do anything he wasn't going to do himself. That put him straight away in a different class from me, Doreen, Len Weatherhead, and the crowd. I heard so much about Billy Crusher, whose name was really Arthur Trubshaw, that one Sunday morning I looked in, out of curiosity, to watch the pair of them training at Weatherhead's gym.

They were already at it when I arrived, so I stood back and watched them. Arthur was a big, powerful chap, but even so he wasn't as strong as Fred. He was much faster and lighter on his feet, with being a trained acrobat and all that, and I could see that he was watching Fred very carefully. He wasn't exactly afraid of him, but he was being very wary. He didn't want any mistakes, because he knew that if Fred should happen to forget the script and let loose that strength of his in the wrong direction, there was every chance of getting hurt. And he wasn't in the business to get hurt, I could see that. He was a clever performer, almost flashy. He knew exactly what he was doing. And his face was unmarked. Nobody had ever taken a swipe at him and broken his nose, and they weren't going to if he could help it.

When I got there, he was showing Fred the way to get out of a lock. The drill was that Arthur got Fred on his back and twisted his legs round in a way that looked bloody agonising to me, but (as I heard Arthur keep telling Fred) wouldn't do him any harm as long as he was expecting it and relaxed. They were to hold this for a bit, while Fred was supposed to writhe about in agony, and then all of a sudden Fred was to draw his knees up and kick out, so that his feet caught Arthur full in the chest and threw him backwards. Then they could go on to the next move. Arthur was pointing out to Fred, very carefully, the exact point on his chest where the feet were to land. No messing about. He didn't want a kick under the heart to make him feel groggy, and neither on the other hand did he want either of the feet to go too high up and get him in the throat. He indicated an exact area and he rehearsed the thing till Fred could have done it in his sleep. Never an inch too high or too low. I was just leaning against the wall, having a smoke and watching the fun, when I heard Len Weatherhead's voice in my ear. "Seem to be getting to know each other all right," he said.

"That chap Arthur'll bring Fred along all right," I said. "He's working very hard on him."

"I should hope he is working hard," said Len, a bit sourly. "He's on full pay during this training period and he doesn't have to fight any bouts. He gets as much for one of these training sessions as he does for a fight in the ring."

Just as he spoke, Fred brought his fist down in the small of Arthur's back. Arthur must have told him to, but perhaps Fred was an inch or two outside the target area, or brought it down too hard, or something. Anyway, Arthur collapsed on the floor, gasping that his kidneys were ruptured and that he was going straight off to his lawyer to sue everybody all round. Fred stood over him, looking apologetic, and Len Weatherhead went over to try to soothe him.

"Bad luck, Arthur," he said, trying to pass it off all cheerful. "Fred'll have to watch what he's doing, won't you, Fred?"

"It looks easy from where you're standing," said Arthur, fixing Len Weatherhead with a very cold eye. His face was white. "I ought to get double pay for this," he said.

"Oh, come on, Arthur," said Len, fencing him off. "You know you do all right."

"All right, is it?" said Arthur, climbing to his feet. "You come and have a bash at it if it's all right."

"What did I do wrong?" Fred puts in, as if he was back at Greenall's and had put some bags of flour in the wrong place or something.

"I'll show you what you did wrong," said Arthur suddenly, and without warning he seized hold of the back of Fred's neck, dragged his head down till he was bent double, and then slammed him in the kidneys with his fist. It made me feel faint to see it. As for Fred, he crumpled up. I thought he was going to be sick. Finally he dragged himself on to his hands and knees, but he couldn't get any further.

"That's what I'm talking about," said Arthur. Really cool he was. "Get that into your head and maybe we'll start making progress."

"Fred," I said through the ropes. "How are you feeling?"

"Don't overdo it, Arthur," said Len Weatherhead.

"He's got to learn," said Arthur. But he sounded a bit nervous, because Fred was climbing to his feet now, with sweat breaking out all over his face, and he didn't like the look in his eyes. None of us did. All his gentleness was gone and his face seemed full of nothing but pain and rage. As I'd noticed before, his huge chest made him seem top-heavy, and as he took a step or two towards Arthur, he seemed to waddle like a gorilla.

Arthur stood his ground, but I noticed that he fell automatically into a wrestler's crouch, ready to defend himself. He sank his head down between his shoulders so that he wouldn't get his neck broken. Just instinct, I suppose. Actually it was all over in a couple of seconds. Len and I both broke into action. He climbed through the ropes and got between them, and at the same time I leaned over and got hold of Fred's arm.

"Don't do it, Fred," I said. "It's me, Bert."

He hadn't realised I was there, and the sound of my voice started him out of his trance. But his mind moved slowly, as usual, and it was like watching a diver come up from the ocean floor.

"He hit me," Fred said to me, as if we were back on the old asphalt playground.

"That's enough for today. Out of the ring," said Len Weatherhead in his manager's voice.

Arthur came over to Fred and looked him straight in the eye. I had to admire his pluck.

"No offence, Fred," he said. "I got a bit rattled when you hit me in the wrong place, that's all. Let's try that again."

I liked him for doing it his own way, ignoring Len Weatherhead's order to break it up for the day. And he was certainly risking something by inviting Fred to give him another punch. But it worked perfectly. They went through three of four movements that looked for all the world like dance steps, and then Fred swung his fist down, and this time it must have been placed right, because although the sound thumped out like somebody kicking a suitcase, Arthur just grinned, and the two of them went off to get dressed.

As I turned away I saw Len Weatherhead staring after them, looking very excited. "I've got a name for him," he said. "Did you see that look that came over his face? Sort of apelike? That's worth a fortune in the ring."

Well, a fortune was a fortune, but Fred was still my brother, so I didn't exactly gush over this discovery of his. "What's the name?" I said, a bit short.

"King Caliban," he said.

"King Who?" I asked. It sounded a bit funny to me.

"Caliban. He was some kind of monster on a desert island, as far as I know. That's the angle to stress, for Fred. The barbaric."

"Why not call him the Missing Link and have done with it?" I asked. But as soon as I'd spoken I wished I hadn't. I could see I'd pushed it too far. If I wanted to stay in with Len, I had to leave him to run his business his own way. He gave me a look that told me pretty clearly that when he wanted my advice he'd ask me for it. So of course I decided to belt up and make myself scarce. I didn't want to spoil everything now that it seemed set fair. I mean to say, it's through playing along with chaps like Len Weatherhead that chaps like me get their place in the sun.

After that, I played it cool for a while. I kept my nose out of it and didn't see anything of Len, or Fred and Doreen, for that matter. Time jogged along and I knew it must be time for Fred and Arthur to have a bout in public, but I didn't think about it much. Then, late one afternoon as I was just locking up the office, Doreen showed up.

"I want you to do me a favour, Bert," she said, coming to the point as usual.

"I know," I said. "Hold Fred's hand when he goes into the ring."

"No, be serious," she said, giving me a very worried look. Her face had gone thin, it seemed to me. Something had frightened her.

"Fred's acting up strange." she said. "Since he gave up Greenall's and gave all his time to practising with Arthur."

"I didn't even know he'd done that," I said.

"Yes, the last three weeks before their first bout," she said. "That was the arrangement. The three weeks'll be up in four days. Mr Weatherhead's been paying him the same wage as he'd have got at Greenall's. Then as soon as he starts having professional fights he'll get the same pay as Arthur."

So he hadn't started to touch the big money yet. Just the worry and the uncertainty.

"Where do I come in?" I asked her.

"Fred doesn't like it," she said. "He's doing it for everybody's sake, but he doesn't like it. And sometimes he seems so strange. I hardly feel I know him any more."

"When he's earning you eighty quid a week," I said, "you won't care whether you know him or not."

"Bert, that's not fair," she said and all of a sudden if she didn't burst out crying. Doreen of all women!

"He frightens me," she said, sobbing so you could hear her in the street. "The other day we had a bit of a difference about the children. I was for telling them about his new job and he said no, let them think he still worked at Greenall's. But they're bound to find out, Fred, I said to him, why not tell them now? Besides, Peter'll be so proud to have a real wrestler for his dad. I was going on like that when all of a sudden he gave a sort of roar. I never heard him make a noise like that before. And he glared at me. His eyes seemed like an animal's. Christ, Bert, I can't explain it. I thought he was going to murder me."

"Did he lay a finger on you?" I asked.

"No," she said.

"Well, then," I said. "If every man who shouted at his wife could scare her as much as you're scared, the world'd be a happier place."

She seemed a bit easier in her mind. After all, there's nothing like having somebody tell you your fears are just imagination. But she hadn't finished with me. She pressed on to the next point.

"Promise you'll come to the fight on Tuesday night, Bert," she said. "I feel I must be there, but I can't stand it by myself."

"Why don't you stay at home?" I said.

"Oh, I couldn't," she said. "I must be with him."

It seemed a funny idea to me. With him. Her and a thousand other people. But I said I'd go. I wasn't keen, but she was anxious and besides, I was curious to see how the act would go over.

I asked Doreen if she'd got any free tickets, and she said no. Somehow, that riveted it. I mean it really convinced me that she *must* be feeling bad about things, to overlook a chance of saving at least fifteen bob.

Anyway, I called for her on the night. She'd asked me to go round at about six, to have a bit of a meal before we set off, and as luck would have it I got there just as Fred was leaving. Len Weatherhead, giving him the V.I.P. treatment, because it was his first bout, had called for him in his Bentley, and Arthur was along too. The three of them were just coming out of the house as I got there, and I must say it looked exactly like a man being arrested by two Scotland Yard detectives. They were jollying him along, and Arthur was even carrying the little suitcase which – I suppose – contained his wrestling outfit. I recognised it. It was his old football case. He used to keep his shorts and boots and things in it, with a little bottle of embrocation. That was when we were between eighteen and twenty-one, both living at home. It made me feel funny to see the old football case going out through the door, on such different business. And there was old Fred. He didn't recognise me. At least, I spoke to him and he looked at me, but he seemed to stare straight through me. His face looked sad and lonely. Yes, *lonely*, as if he'd spent about five years in a desert and given up hope of ever meeting another human being.

Well, I thought, the first time is always uphill, whatever it is you're doing. He'll settle down. I went on into the house and there was Doreen with the children. She'd got some sort of game out on the table, a jigsaw or something and was trying to get them interested in it, to cover up for Fred. But she wasn't having much luck. They could tell there was something going on, and they both kept asking where Dad was till it nearly drove her nuts.

We ate some kippers, neither of us saying anything much, and then the neighbour who was going to mind the kids came in and we got into our coats and on our way. In the car I started trying to raise Doreen's spirits a bit. "As of tonight," I said to her, "you and Fred can kiss your worries good-bye. A solid fifty to eighty quid a week in the season, and he can always go back to humping groceries when his reactions begin to slow down and he can't wrestle any longer. You're a very lucky girl," I told her.

"But if it's going to make Fred different," she whined, but I cut her short. I wasn't having any of that. "Different, my foot," I said. "It's just exchanging one trade for another that's a bit worrying at first. This isn't fighting. It's an acrobatic display, and Fred's been well trained for it. It's the chance of a lifetime. Considering he isn't overburdened with grey matter, this kind of thing is the only kind of work he can be trained for."

She quietened down a bit, but when we got to the Town Hall and saw the crowd streaming in, she got all upset again, and to tell the truth I didn't feel any too good myself. The faces! They seemed like things you'd see in an nightmare. I didn't know which were the worst, the men or the women. There were women of all ages, from old grandmothers down to teenagers, and they all had that bright-eyed look that people wear when they're going to see something really horrible. *To see a man get beaten up and hurt –* that was what they were there for, and it was as plain as if they'd had it on sandwich boards. Perhaps they'd all been ill treated by a man at some time or other. Perhaps every woman has. Well, I thought, at least the all-in game is one that won't lack support. The cinemas can close, the dog-tracks can close, but this'll keep going. Fred's on to a good thing, I told myself. But I wasn't too happy inside.

The usual flourishing and announcing went on, and then the first bout started. It was between a character covered from head to foot in red tights, with just little holes for his eyes, and another chap who'd gone to the other extreme and was nearly naked. The red one was called the Scarlet Fiend or the Red Devil or something. He was the one the crowd were supposed to be against, though as far as I could see they were both equally horrible and when it came to fighting dirty, hitting the other chap when he wasn't looking and the rest of it, there was nothing to choose. But the crowd were there for thrills, and they started to get worked up straight away. The girls! screaming advice, too. Where they picked it up I don't know. The worst was a big bald-headed fellow about four seats away from me. We were in the third row from the ringside, and I could see that if they'd been ringside seats this chap would have had his head through the ropes to shout at the wrestlers better. He seemed completely beside himself. He wanted to see murder committed. Nothing short of complete bestiality would satisfy him. He must have been some kind of pervert like you read about in the Sunday paper. He never stopped shouting from the first minute to the last. And when the action really got hot, he'd leap to his feet and start dancing about with excitement, till the people behind him had to grab him and pull him down again, so they could see.

I saw Doreen glancing at this bald chap once or twice, and I could tell what she was thinking. If he shouted like that when Fred was fighting, she wasn't going to be able to stand it. I made a little joke about him, trying to get her to see him as funny, but I couldn't put my heart into it. I didn't think he was funny myself, that was the trouble. So I concentrated on the money. "It's worth it for eighty quid," I said to Doreen. She gave me an expressionless look and I couldn't tell what was going on in her mind.

We watched three or four more bouts and I began to feel numb. My sense of proportion came back and I thought, well, it's just a lot of silly fools shouting and getting worked up. "All in the day's work," I said to Doreen. She gave me the same look again.

I got so sunk in my thoughts that I hardly watched the ring any more, and it shook me to hear all of a sudden the name "Billy Crusher" shouted out by the M.C. He went on to tell the fans that he was matched tonight with the most dangerous opponent he had ever faced, a new import never before seen in any ring in the civilised world, an untamed giant straight from the jungle. And there they were climbing into the ring, and the M.C. was bawling, "KING CALIBAN!"

As soon as I saw the two of them up there I knew how it was going to be slanted. Arthur had those flashy good looks, especially when you saw him from a few yards away, with the arc lights shining down on the smooth torso of his. The idol of the gallery. Especially the women. Fred, by contrast, would have looked pretty lumpy and plain anyway, and to make it worse they'd dressed him in a leopard skin so that he looked like a jungle chieftain in a B picture. I don't think they'd actually used grease-paint on him, but it's a fact that his face looked much uglier than I'd ever seen it before. Perhaps it was just the angle at which I was looking up at him. But his forehead seemed narrow and sloping. I don't think I'd have recognised him if I hadn't known.

The crowd were well away by now, having witnessed half a dozen crimes of violence already, and they started barracking poor old Fred straight away, calling him all sorts of names, and telling Arthur to throttle him and put a stop to his career. I knew Fred was supposed to feed all this by reacting and making all sorts of threatening gestures, but he just stood there looking lonely, as if he was still wandering in that solitary desert. It made him seem sub-human, like a bear that had been brought in to be baited. I glanced at Doreen. She had her head bent and was staring down at her feet. I knew she wouldn't look at the ring.

The fight started and they went pretty smoothly into the routine. Arthur's training had been good, and I was hoping they'd get through without any accidents and finish with it, so that I could take Doreen home. Then when she had Fred back with her, plus a big fat pay-packet, things would seem rosier. This was the low ebb, having to sit there and watch them twist one another's limbs.

The bald chap seemed to have taken a real dislike to Fred, and he was hooting insults at him right from the start, rejoicing whenever Arthur looked like maiming him, and groaning like a stuck pig when Fred was on top. I nearly leaned over and asked him to shut up, but it wouldn't have done any good. He was demented. I think he wanted to attract Fred's attention, to have him come to the ropes and shake his fist or threaten to come down and do him. That's what those nut cases want – to be in on the act. "Serve you right!" he'd scream, whenever Fred got jumped on or twisted. "That's what you need!" I could see it was making Doreen sick, and I felt a bit dicky myself.

What was worse, I could see that Baldy was beginning to rattle Fred. His voice was very penetrating, and it must have got in through Fred's insulation, so to speak. Every time he was taking punishment, to hear that screech right in his ear – it was enough to send him round the bend, if he hadn't been half-way there already.

At one point, after they'd done a very clever double fall which ended with Fred being thrown up in the air and landing on his back, Baldy set up such a howl of glee that Fred turned on one elbow and looked at him. He could see who was doing the shouting, and he gave him the same look that I'd seen him give Arthur in the gym that morning. His sub-human look. I felt myself break into a sweat. If that was how he'd looked at Doreen no wonder she was frightened. He slowly got to his feet, still glaring at Baldy, then slowly he turned to face Arthur, who was waiting to get on with the act.

From that moment on, Fred's performance went to pieces. His timing went off and he seemed to be acting in a dream. He was so much slower than Arthur that Arthur had to keep waiting for him, and it began to look obvious. I saw Arthur's lips moving and I could see he was whispering to Fred, trying to get him to snap it up. Then, suddenly, Fred made a bad mistake. He put the wrong lock on Arthur and really hurt him. Arthur twisted away, and with the same quick flash of temper as I'd seen him show before, he dug his elbow savagely into Fred's ribs. It was more petulant than anything else – a kind of reminder to keep his mind on the job. But it was too much. Fred must have seen red. He swung round and slapped Arthur across the side of the head with his open hand. It made him reel across the ring. And before anyone could stop them, they were fighting. It was the strangest thing I ever saw, the way they switched from mock fighting to real in a couple of seconds. They were both mad and out to hurt each other.

Naturally that didn't last long. The ref. saw what was going on, and moved in to break it up. But at that moment Arthur got a punch in that went under Fred's ribs and made him gasp for breath. He stood there for a moment, fighting for breath, and at that moment I saw his face. It was quite calm, just very lonely. As if he'd gone beyond anyone's power to help him or speak to him.

It was all over in a moment. Fred pushed the ref. away, turned to Arthur and suddenly swung a fist in the air, like a club, then crashed it down on Arthur's skull. The whole place fell silent. Everybody knew this was not fooling. Arthur lurched, tried to put his hands up to his head, then fell forward. I remember thinking, "He's killed him." I still don't know, for that matter. He's still unconscious but he may get better.

I told you a lie. I said the whole place fell silent. But there was one still on his feet and shouting. Yes. The bald chap. He was pointing a finger straight at Fred and screaming, "Dirty! A foul! He fouled him!" Nobody else was moving or making a sound, but Baldy couldn't stop yelling. I suppose he was hysterical.

Then, like a nightmare, I saw Fred come across the ring and through the ropes. I tried to call to him, but my throat was dry and nothing came out. I knew at once what he was going to do. The people on the front row scattered as he walked straight over them. And the second row. The ref. jumped down and tried to scramble after him. Doreen was screaming. But it was too late, he'd got hold of the bald chap and was lifting him above his head like a log of wood. Higher and higher he lifted him. My voice came back and I cried, "Don't do it, Fred! Don't do it!"

But he did it. He flung the man down across the wooden seats, as if it was the seats he hated and he was using the man's body to break them with.

Don't ask me how we got out of there. Of course the police were there within five minutes. They got Fred into a Black Maria even before they got the bald chap into an ambulance. As far as I can make out, he'll live. So it all might have been worse. Of course I feel a bit shaken. I spent the night on the settee at Doreen's, after the police let me go. But I didn't sleep. And I haven't felt up to doing anything all day. As I said to them, that's what happens when you try to help anybody. Well, it's a lesson to me. Let them get on with it from now on.

Doreen's telephoned to say that Fred's been asking for me. Well, let him ask. He got himself into this, let him get himself out. I mean to say, all right, it was my idea for him to go in for wrestling. But how was I to know he'd do a bloody silly thing like that?

And what am I going to say to Len Weatherhead when I meet him?

I Love You, Ricky

As Hilda came along the street, her satchel heavy across her shoulder, she saw Elizabeth and Rodney, in the distance, waiting by the gate for her.

Hilda slowed down and stopped, her heart pounding. Of course she knew what it was all about. The cufflink! She set down her satchel on the ground and stood perfectly still. Her body felt soft and vulnerable: so soft, so female, so inexperienced in dealing with trouble. And this was terrible trouble. Once started, it would go on for ever, spoiling everything in her life.

Elizabeth was Hilda's friend. At fifteen, she was older than Hilda by one year and dominated her in everything. Tall and dark, with pink cheeks, she had left school and started in an office where the male workers had already started to ask her out in the evenings. Hilda, on her family's insistence, was still at school, would still be at school in a year's time when she reached Elizabeth's age. (But Elizabeth, having moved on another year, would still be mockingly out of reach.) In spite of these disparities, the girls were "friends", because they lived in the same road, in identical houses, and swooned over the same pop records.

Their favourite pop star was Ricky. Once, nearly a year ago, they had been together to hear Ricky perform. He had a way of bending backwards from the knees as if about to get under a wire fence, throwing his head back and singing in jerks through his nose. The effect was like that of an enormous rooster crowing. Perhaps because of this, both girls were passionately in love with him. They had crushed into a huge, barn-like cinema with thousands of other girls, all equally inflamed by Ricky's rooster-performance, and afterwards they had hurried round to the stage-door. There, blind with adoration, they had thrown themselves into the clawing, screaming mass of girls who were trying to break the police cordon and get at Ricky.

Standing still by someone's garden hedge, Hilda nearly fainted as she recalled that moment. Ricky had come out of the building, head down and hurrying. The thin screams had risen in volume to a wild, awful yelling. Suddenly, among the forest of hands that groped towards Ricky, trying to tear off scraps of his clothing, one hand had closed like steel on the young hero's elegant shirt-cuff. With a wrench, the police had dragged him on, towards the sanctuary of his waiting car. But the girl, shrieking, had held up her trophy – a beautiful topaz cufflink. No sooner was the shriek out than a dozen hands grabbed for the prize. And the hand that got it was Elizabeth's. Hilda remembered the fierce, set look on Elizabeth's face as she grabbed the cufflink and buffeted a way through the crowd. Ricky was her man, and nothing – no person, no scruple, no hesitation or weakening – was going to come between her and her man. The girl who had first taken the cufflink was sobbing, trying to fight her way through the crowd after Elizabeth's disappearing head and shoulders, but it was hopeless; no one would have helped her, since any girl who managed to wrest the cufflink from Elizabeth would have kept it for herself.

When, finally, they managed to catch the bus home with the cufflink secretly stowed away, the pair were as radiant as successful jewel-thieves.

"All's fair in love and war," Hilda said to herself, muttering the words into the quiet suburban air. But if all was fair, then she must not complain now that it must come to open war between her and Elizabeth. War? But she had no weapons. She could only suffer, and endure, for Ricky's sake.

It was all too clear what must have happened. As she moved on, step by step approaching the explosion, she brought Rodney's twelve-year-old face into focus. Her little brother. He was wearing the triumphant jeer that meant he had found a way of hurting her. She wondered, fleetingly, whether it would be possible to kill him. A knife? She wouldn't have the nerve. The thought of how it would feel as the blade forced its way between Rodney's ribs, severing flesh and fat, plunging into his black, beating heart . . . she gave a feminine shudder. Girls didn't do things like that. She was a girl, and she loved Ricky, and she must suffer for her love, as women had always suffered.

But had women like Elizabeth suffered? Hadn't they simply gone ahead and got what they wanted and then enjoyed it? Hilda slowed down again, almost stopped. She could see both their faces clearly now. Elizabeth's was closed, narrow with hate, her lips compressed into a hair-line. Rodney's was shining with pure joy. I'm glad someone's happy, she thought bitterly.

Halting again, feeling the stir of spring in the gardens and the hopefulness of green things pushing up, indifferent to her wild misery, Hilda saw in her mind's eye, with the sudden emphatic clarity of a series of woodcuts, the steps of her downfall.

It had started soon after the triumphant cufflink-snatching. With a bold persistence that surprised her at herself, Hilda had claimed a share.

"You ought to let me keep it part of the time. I was with you."

Elizabeth was outraged. "You were with me? What difference did that make?"

"You'd never have got it without me. I supported you."

"*Supported* me?"

"Egged you on. You know I did."

Elizabeth's pretty pink cheeks turned quite pale with astonishment. "I know nothing of the kind. You must have gone mad."

"I *haven't*. I'm being quite reasonable. That cufflink of Ricky's is partly mine and I ought to have it some of the time."

"But it *isn't* yours. Not one bit of it is yours."

"I helped you to get it."

The quiet, intense wrangle continued through many evenings. At last Elizabeth, to her own secret amazement, found herself crumbling before the utter single-mindedness of Hilda's advance.

"Tell you what. We'll say it's a tenth yours and you can keep it one week in ten."

"It's at least one third mine and I want it one week in three."

Finally they settled that Hilda should have the cufflink one week in four.

From then on, this pattern of three-and-one became the rhythm of Hilda's life. Her three weeks of dispossession were a dry, aching desert in every month, to be got through only by a devoted patience and dedication. Up in her bedroom, she played Ricky's records over and over again, and talked (quietly, so that Rodney should not hear her through the door if he were eavesdropping) to the big glossy photograph of Ricky she had framed, with her own hands, and hung on the wall where she could best see it from her bed. "I'm waiting, Ricky," she told him. "Only another eleven days and then I'll be touching something you've touched. Then we'll be together."

And when the golden one week in four arrived, when Elizabeth –precisely at twelve noon on the Saturday – ungraciously handed over the relic in its nest of tissue paper – Hilda's happiness bloomed like a desert flower. Hurrying to her room, she would start the turntable moving, and a record of Ricky's, specially chosen to fit her exact mood of that day, would crash out: sweet, throbbing rooster-voice triumphantly riding the torrent of rhythm-section and echo chamber. Abandoning herself blissfully to Ricky's presence, Hilda would lie on her bed, staring at the photograph of her loved one, listening to his voice, and clasping his cufflink to her heart.

In all this felicity, she feared only one enemy: Rodney, whose life was governed by a few simple, unargued assumptions, one of them being that he was his elder sister's natural enemy. He was willing to devote any quantity of time and energy to spying on Hilda, implacably pursuing her, probing for the slightest sign of a weakness he could exploit in order to cause her pain and loss. He showed no slackening of enthusiasm for this self-appointed task, and no signs of surfeit when, as sometimes happened, he managed to get her at a real disadvantage and torment her without mercy. For her part, she accepted him and his fiendish young-brotherdom as one of life's unavoidable evils, like homework or the dentist. One thing she was sure of. Rodney must never, never, *never* get his hands on Ricky's cufflink. He knew there was something going on between her and Elizabeth, some arrangement that involved a precious object, but his most determined prying had so far yielded nothing. Hilda never gave herself over to worship of Ricky without locking her door and stuffing the keyhole with cotton-wool, which she then fastened with adhesive tape so that Rodney could not poke it out with a knitting-needle or some similar instrument. She knew him! While she was at school, the cufflink lay in a locked drawer, and the room was locked as well. The thought of Rodney's pudgy, scornful hands handling, resting on, so much as coming *near* anything that had been Ricky's, filled her with agitation and loathing.

All this was present to Hilda's mind as she stood now, in the afternoon sunshine, longing to run away but knowing it was useless to try to evade her approaching destruction. And even in this moment of dreadful confrontation, she recognised the justice of her fate. She had tempted the gods. She had drawn down this catastrophe on her own head. With the secret complicity of Ricky, she had entered on the path of crime. For his sake, she had set aside all earthly laws. She loved him so much that nothing could stand in the path of her love.

To be precise, it had been during her eighth week of possession, eight long months since the cufflink had been so daringly wrenched from its moorings, that the idea occurred to her, the idea that had made her, for Ricky's sake, a criminal. It had come in two stages; first, *Elizabeth's love for Ricky is shallow compared with mine. No one else knows how to love as I do: utterly, consumingly, daring and sacrificing all:* second, *Elizabeth does not deserve Ricky's cufflink.* In a blinding flash, leaving her weak and dissolving, the directive came: *Pretend to have lost it.*

Promptly that evening she went to Elizabeth and confessed. The tears, the storming vituperation on one side, the endless explanations, apologies, cries of penitence on the other! Elizabeth, hard-eyed, had demanded access to Hilda's room; Hilda, who had predicted this (in a matter so crucial, there could be no question of trust between them), at once agreed, and submissively helped Elizabeth to scrutinise drawers, cupboards, the very mattress and pillow-case; finally, with a new emotional storm, the search was declared hopeless.

"How *could* you?" Elizabeth kept saying, helplessly. "How *could* you be so careless with it?"

"I keep telling you. I took it to school in my satchel. Someone must have – "

"How could you be so *silly*? I expect you talked to all your silly little friends about it and passed it round in class."

"Of *course* I didn't. Not a living soul knew I had it, except you. And it was in the *strongest* compartment of my satchel – I just don't understand – '

The scene dragged on for hours. At last, pale and exhausted, Elizabeth took herself off. Somehow, during the weeks that followed, she forced herself to accept the situation. Ricky's cufflink was gone, she would never again touch it and enjoy that thrilling vicarious contact with his tanned, manly skin. Hilda had lost it: Hilda, who had doggedly beaten down her instinctive resistance to parting with it, and with the same doggedness established the semblance of a right to possession of it – she, this Hilda, had lost the cufflink and plunged both their lives into darkness. But Hilda's darkness was not so profound as hers: it could not be. Her manner towards Hilda grew cool and distant; they met rarely. Friendship is weaker than love.

Meanwhile, under her mask of penitence, Hilda glowed with a dark, fiery pleasure. Cradling the cufflink in her hands, she lay on her bed, her toes crinkling to the rhythm of Ricky's voice as it poured over her from the record-player, and stared up at his picture: that great solitary picture, stately on the uncluttered wall. (Elizabeth showed the essential vulgarity of her nature by the fact that *her* room was papered, over every inch, with hundreds of photographs of Ricky. She plastered up every picture she could lay hands on, good, bad or mediocre. That was mere collecting, mere possessiveness, whereas Hilda's one big glossy picture was *worship*.) As Hilda gazed up at Ricky, he seemed to be gazing down at her, and in his eyes she read understanding and sympathy. He knew that she had lied, betrayed and stolen – for his sake.

"Nothing matters but you, Ricky," she told him. "I'd do *anything*."

And as his voice enveloped her, and his cufflink lay in her hand, she swooned deliciously into thoughts of his nearness. This was living: the world was rich, gay, mad, and she had bought it, like Faust, with a huge, secret sin.

After each of these sessions, she returned the cufflink to its hiding-place. And each time she felt a thrill of pride in having found the perfect concealment. Hilda had a bicycle. The bicycle had fat rubber handlebar-grips. One of the handlebar-grips was loose enough to pull off. She pulled it off, tucked the cufflink into the tubular steel, and pushed the grip back into place. Rodney might search her saddle-bag; probably he did so mechanically, two or three times a week, in a routine search for any fragment he could pick up and use against her. But he would be unlikely to touch the handlebar-grips, much less pull them off, unless he actually got on the bicycle and rode it. And this he would never do. He had a bicycle of his own, a male bicycle, and he would not so much as balance himself on a female bicycle for fear of seeming girlish.

Now forcing her feet to tread forward in a straight line, measuring every step as if moving towards her newly dug grave, Hilda went to meet Elizabeth and Rodney. There was no hope in her heart. She knew they must have found the cufflink. Nothing else would account for their alliance – for Elizabeth normally viewed Rodney with lofty indifference – or for the expressions on their faces as they waited for her.

She drew near. Neither of her enemies moved or spoke. The air seemed unnaturally still, as if crammed with lethal thunder awaiting its moment to break out.

She halted in front of them, not speaking. One of Elizabeth's hands was clenched. Now, slowly and with a gesture full of accusation, she opened it. The cufflink lay in her palm. Its topaz stones, never so beautiful before or afterwards, gathered up the afternoon with their heavy translucency.

Hilda's voice was dry and flat, like the creak of a hinge, as she said: "Where did you find it?"

"He gave it me," said Elizabeth. She nodded her head towards Rodney, but without taking her accusing eyes from Hilda's eyes.

Rodney said contentedly, "My bike had a puncture and I had to get to an important team match, so I borrowed yours."

He had overcome his fear of being thought effeminate in his even greater fear of missing some foolish, trivial, accursed game. And his reward was a triumph over Hilda greater than anything he had dreamt of.

"But how did you know what it was, when you found it?" Hilda persisted dully.

"Oh, I knew about your soppy cufflink," he said with amused contempt. "I heard Mum talking to Elizabeth's mum about it." He laughed, sneeringly, extracting every drop of pleasure from the moment, triumphing over both of them.

Oblivious of him, the two girls looked at each other. There was nothing to say. The situation was beyond comment. Slowly, Elizabeth put the cufflink away in her handbag. Then, before turning her back, she spoke.

"Don't expect me ever to speak to you again."

Rapidly, firmly, she walked away before Hilda could reply. In any case, what was there to say? All that was left to her was to get away before Rodney could rub any more salt into her wound. He must not see how much he had hurt her. One day, one day, she would find some way of hurting him as much. She would wait, she would watch, she would give her whole life to it if necessary.

She hurried upstairs, unlocked her room, entered, locked it again, made sure the cotton-wool was securely taped in the key-hole; then, and only then, did she allow herself to sink down on the bed. No tears came: the picture of Ricky stared down into her dry, dilated eyes.

The record-player? Would it be a help to hear his voice? No – she shuddered away from the prospect. She knew, with a cold, constricting intuition, how it would sound: unfriendly, accusing. Great crimes are joyous only if they succeed. To cheat and steal for Ricky was fine. But to cheat and steal and be found out – that was failure. And there was no place for failure in his young and shining face.

Hilda knew what she must do. Sadly, she got up from her bed, went over to the wall and took down the resplendent picture of Ricky. Then she went to her record cabinet and took out his records. She had half-a-dozen in all. Placing these on the photograph in a neat pile, she went to her dressing-table and found her prettiest silk scarf. She wrapped the records and the photograph in the scarf, making a neat bundle which she then fastened with ribbon.

For a moment, Hilda stood with the silk-wrapped parcel in her hand, as if estimating its weight. Then, with a sudden resolution, she opened the bottom drawer, lifted up the clothes that were in it, and hid the parcel away underneath everything. She shut the drawer. Ricky's voice and face lay hidden under vests and pullovers, like roots sleeping in the winter earth.

Moving slowly, as if hypnotised, Hilda pulled the adhesive tape away from the keyhole and took out the cotton-wool, which she dropped into the waste-paper-basket. With her hand on the doorknob, she stood for a moment looking round at her room. Without Ricky's picture on the wall, without the cotton-wool in the keyhole, it was no longer a refuge. It was just a room like any other. And her life, now, was just a life like any other: a vast, level desert stretching away without interruption from this moment until her last heart-beat.

She went out on to the landing and down the stairs. Rodney, who had been sitting in his own room with the door ajar, saw her and grinned to himself. He had been busy polishing a few phrases about soppy girls who stole things from people who had stolen them in the first place and thus made themselves thieves twice over. And also sketching out a brilliant series of sarcastic references to handlebars. His face shining with happiness, he got to his feet and followed his sister down the stairs.

Christmas at Rillingham's

"You know, Sidney," Mr Rillingham said in a loud voice, "Patty is a very lucky girl."

The reason he spoke loudly was not because Sidney was a long way away. Sidney was right next to him, helping him to arrange some new gramophones in the big window. It was because Patty was a long way away, and what was more she had a record going, as usual.

Sidney knew it did not make any difference to Mr Rillingham whether he answered or not, so he just nodded and said, "Lucky."

"Fancy anybody getting so much fun out of what they do for a living!" Mr Rillingham said, still loudly.

"Doesn't seem right," said Sidney, bending to pick up a display card he had knocked over.

"Mind you, I've nothing against it," said Mr Rillingham. "Quite the reverse. It does my heart good to see anyone happy! Particularly anybody young and lovely, eh, Sidney?"

"Cor, yes," said Sidney, as if he were talking to himself.

"Young, lovely, and happy," said Mr Rillingham. A wall of sound moved up from the other end of the shop and knocked his words back into his mouth. Sidney could imagine them curling round his large teeth like blown pieces of paper round lamp-posts and railings.

"Each night I ask – the stars erp aber-her-herve:
Why merst I be – a teen-eh-eyger in lerve?"

"Beg pardon, Mr Rillingham?" Patty called down the length of the shop. "Did you say somethink?"

"I was just remarking to Sidney here," Mr Rillingham answered, raising his voice above the swelling uproar, "that you're a very lucky girl."

"Roll on death," said Sidney quietly to himself.

"Well, don't I deserve to be?" said Patty, coming towards them. "After all, it's Christmas." She halted about six feet away from Mr Rillingham, who was kneeling inside the big window with his jacket off, and gave him an arch smile.

Mr Rillingham did not answer. He seemed slightly embarrassed. Sidney had noticed before that Mr Rillingham liked to be facetiously flirtatious with Patty as long as they were at opposite ends of the shop and as long as he, Sidney, could be brought in as insulating material. But if Patty came close up to Mr Rillingham and gave him the face-to-face treatment, it seemed to make him curl up.

She had round, staring blue eyes and fair hair cut close to her head. Sidney did not consider her face very beautiful, so he generally kept his eyes on her figure, which was of the type that suggests words like "opulent" and "generous". To put it bluntly, her breasts were so big that Sidney had at first concluded that she must have padded them out. Of late, however, he had begun to think that they must be genuine, but opportunities for verification seemed slow in coming along. Altogether the situation was one that fatigued Sidney very thoroughly.

"Seems about all right, boss," Sidney said, looking down at the four shiny record-players, of different sizes and styles, that they had arranged.

"Should be," said Mr Rillingham, straightening up with re-lieved briskness. "I'll go outside and see." He clambered out of the window and went out through the shop door, putting on his jacket as he went.

"Bit late to be putting that lot on show, twenty-fourth," said Patty.

"Just come in," Sidney explained. "Besides, it'd surprise you how many grams and other big stuff get sold right up to closing time Christmas Eve. Families get all set for the Christmas binge, then the young ones come home and say 'No! Not still using the *old* type record-player?' The old man comes around here with his pockets bursting with Christmas money and wham! Before you know, we've sold three, four gramophones on Christmas Eve afternoon!"

"Uh huh," Patty answered. She was moving her mouth rhyth-mically, as if chewing a piece of gum, and watching Mr Rillingham standing outside on the pavement like a customer.

Sidney wondered why he bothered to talk to Patty. He never struck a natural tone with her. His feelings towards her were too confused.

Mr Rillingham, outside on the pavement, gave a last critical glance to the big window, went round the corner to look at the small one, and came back to the shop door. He was just opening it when a party of young people, two youths and two girls, all in duffle jackets and slacks, surged round the corner and jostled through the door. They did not appear to see Mr Rillingham, though they all but pushed him out of the way in their triumphant assault on the shop door. Sidney had a glimpse of Mr Rillingham's face, red and glaring with anger, through the glass of the door. Then the young people flooded into the shop, seeming to fill it with noise, restless limbs, coloured scarves and gloves, and the name "Patty". It was as if a party had started up in the shop.

Sidney watched Mr Rillingham walk slowly into the shop, shut the door behind him and stand for a moment looking at the five young people clustered round the record display at the far end. As he watched, the annoyance faded from his face and it creased into a pudgy smile.

"Best thing I ever did for the business, Sidney," said Mr Rillingham fondly.

"Made a difference," said Sidney.

"It's the young people that have got the money today, Sidney," said Mr Rillingham. "Our disc trade'd be nothing without the young people."

"Thirty-four," said Sidney under his breath.

"Rock and roll!" said Mr Rillingham joyously. "Long life to it!"

"Many happy returns," said Sidney.

"So everybody's happy," said Mr Rillingham. "A very nice thing to be able to say at Christmas time! Patty likes selling this type of line, she can talk to the customers about it! She's as much a fan as they are!"

"Silly cow," said Sidney within himself.

"You know how many pictures of Elvis Presley she has at home, that girl?" Mr Rillingham demanded, wheeling on Sidney.

"Pretty fair, I expect," said Sidney, flicking about him with a duster.

"*Ninety*," said Mr Rillingham solemnly. "All different. So she tells me, and I believe her. I tell you she's *mad* on that stuff."

"Mad's right," said Sidney, before he could stop himself. Mr Rillingham frowned.

"Mad or not, young man," he said, his tone changing in an instant, "it's enthusiasm that sells a line, makes it move off the shelves. Why do these young people come in here rather than another shop? Because of Patty. And why because of Patty?"

"To look at her big knockers," Sidney wanted to say. But he knew that Mr Rillingham's reason was the true one.

"They like a saleslady that understands their tastes. Why, she'll play records with 'em for hours and never worry if they go out at the end of it without buying a one. And I don't worry either! It doesn't do a record any harm to be played a few times. And then when the day comes that they *have* got some money...Ha!" Mr Rillingham breathed, wrapped in a beatific vision of expanding and still expanding business. "They come here because they remember the good time they had with Patty playing rock and roll to them all afternoon and never asking them to buy one!"

"And that time does come, Sidney," Mr Rillingham added sharply, as if remembering that he was giving Sidney a pep-talk. "It always does come. Because it's the young people to-day, in the world we're living in, that have got the money."

"Thirty-five," Sidney counted quietly.

"Got mahself a sleepum talkn' cryn' walkn' LIVIN' DAHL," shouted the gramophone above the whinnying of the adolescents.

The telephone rang, and Mr Rillingham moved across to answer it. Sidney was glad to be left alone for a moment, to swallow down his bad temper. He began savagely polishing a record cabinet with his duster. Why did Mr Rillingham have to come every five minutes and tell him, Sidney, what a lot of good Patty was doing the business? Sidney was not even on the sales side; he was training to be a radio and TV technician. Already he had quite a responsible job, driving the van round and delivering sets and installing them; he could repair most things and was going to evening classes and studying for a diploma. He wasn't interested in standing behind a counter and playing tomfool rock-and-roll discs for a lot of giggling kids in duffle coats. Why did Mr Rillingham feel it necessary to tell *him*, Sidney, thirty-five separate times, that the young people were the ones with the money nowadays?

As for Patty, Sidney considered her a big phony. He was pretty sure, for one thing, that they called her "Pat" at home. He would take a bet that she had started calling herself Patty because it was the kind of name that went with pop and rock. No doubt if she had written it down she would have spelt it with an "i", "Patti". Sidney decided that what she needed was to be taken over someone's knee and have her bottom spanked. At the same time, being an honest boy and always ready to own up to base motives, he admitted to himself that it would be nice to have a girl like Patty for a bit of the old you-know-what. It was a pity she did not seem to go for him at all. They would have been just right, especially for age, he being eighteen and she seventeen. Sidney felt sad, and without warning a heavy sigh escaped him.

"Yes, we're ready, Sam," Mr Rillingham was saying into the telephone. His voice sounded pleased and excited. "I've got it okayed by the Post Office. Bring it round whenever you like. We're all ready."

He hung up and walked off to his desk at the back of the shop. Sidney thought how typical this was. If there was anything really to say, Mr Rillingham never bothered to tell Sidney till the last minute. Whereas, on the other hand, Sidney was quite good enough to be chattered to, especially about Patty. The fact was that Mr Rillingham liked talking to himself, but didn't want to admit it because of seeming eccentric, so he made a show of talking to Sidney.

The adolescents were in a spending mood. They played a dozen records and bought nearly all of them. Patty was leaning against the counter, tapping her foot and singing the lyrics. Sidney could hear her even above the racket, because she sang exactly to the rhythm but not quite exactly to the key. In this way she achieved the maximum grating effect on Sidney's nerves. She knew all the records by heart and never made a mistake: for instance, if a singer gave the word "love" three wobbles so that it came out as "ler-her-herve", Patty did exactly the same, neither a wobble less nor a wobble more. She gasped and gulped in all the right places; it was quite an accomplishment. Only she did not seem to have any sense of pitch.

The kids went out with their records in Christmas paper under their arms, and for a moment the shop was quiet. Mr Rillingham called over from his desk: "What're you on now, Sidney?"

"Got to get this job wired up," Sidney called. "Then I'm free. Thought I'd go out and get the – "

"Just stay where I can see you for five minutes," said Mr Rillingham, as if Sidney were a mischievous child. "They're bringing something round from Mayhew's wholesale that I want to show you and Patty."

"Something to show us!" said Patty, overdoing the girlish excitement. "Something for Christmas!"

"Yes, something for Christmas," said Mr Rillingham, smiling carelessly. "A Christmas present to the shop."

"Oh – the shop!" She pouted with magenta lips. "How does the *shop* know it's Christmas?"

"Never mind, Patty," said Mr Rillingham, leaving his desk

and coming forward. "The shop isn't the only one that's going to get a Christmas treat, is it?"

Sidney, watching intently from the corner of his eye, saw Patty glance up sharply as if to caution Mr Rillingham, who stopped talking and looked for a moment as if he could have bitten his tongue off. This led Sidney to analyse the last sentence Mr Rillingham had spoken. It seemed harmless enough, except for that concluding "is it?" To tell the girl she was going to get a Christmas treat was one thing, but "is it?" suggested that there was something afoot between them.

Sidney thought of Mr Rillingham's wife, who was like a jowly old bulldog. At one time Mrs Rillingham had come to the shop nearly every day, but a few months ago Mr Rillingham had bought a new house, out in the country, and now she came very seldom, the bus service not being good.

"We need all these ordering, Mr Rillingham," said Patty in a bright business-girl voice, handing a list to her employer. "We're getting quite low on EP's. You wouldn't believe how the Cliff Richards have been going! And we shall be needing replacements for the Nat King Coles and a lot of new cha-cha-cha."

Cha-cha-cha, thought Sidney bitterly. I'd like to give you ruddy cha-cha-cha. And him old enough to be your ruddy father. "Roll on death," he said to himself, quite loudly.

The shop door pinged, and two men came in. The first was red-faced Mr Mayhew, a crony of Mr Rillingham's; behind him came one of his employees with a bulky piece of apparatus in his arms.

"Hello, Sam!" Mr Rillingham shouted. "No, leave it there, by the telephone!" Smiling plumply, he danced down the shop.

A middle-aged man, staring about him morosely, came in to buy some pop records to play in his cafeteria. He went down to Patty's counter, but before she could get involved in a new piece of business Mr Rillingham called to her, "Patty, just let the gentleman look through the discs by himself a minute, if he wouldn't mind. And come up here, will you please? I've got something to show you. And you, Sidney," he added.

They all clustered round the apparatus, which Mr Mayhew's man was attaching to the telephone. "Comes on and off quite easy, see," said the man. "Watch this, watch this, Sidney," said Mr Rillingham impatiently. "I shall expect you to service it." "I seen 'em before," said Sidney carelessly; he had not, but he felt something was due to his dignity. Amid chatter and exclamations, the installation went on.

"Oo! What is it?" Patty bubbled.

"Telephone-answering device," said Sidney tersely. Mr Rillingham looked at him angrily for stealing this small piece of thunder.

"Yes, you see, Patty," he said with a fatherly smile, "when the shop's closed, we can have the telephone answered by this tape-recorder. It greets the customer, he says what he wants, and the tape records it! Then we play it back when we come in! It's like – like an unsleeping secretary," he finished impressively.

"Big White Deal," said Sidney under his breath.

"Right, thassit," said Mr Mayhew's man, who seemed anxious to wash his hands of the whole affair. "Speak the words in 'ere, guv," he said, holding the microphone up to Mr Rillingham.

"Ah, no," said Mr Rillingham archly. He was so excited about the telephone-answering device that he was quite forgetting to be discreet. "The customers won't want to hear my voice. They'll want to hear a nice young lady's voice."

"Oo, go on," said Patty. She was quite forgetting, too. She was also forgetting, as Sidney sardonically noticed, to act like a girl whose name was Patty or Patti. It was girls called Pat who said things like "Oo, go on."

"Now, listen carefully, Patty," said Mr Rillingham. He was controlling himself, keeping his voice calm as befitted a successful business man, and only the sparkle of his eyes showed how hugely, almost insanely, he was enjoying himself. "You're going to record the message. Now, repeat after me: this is Rillingham's Television, Radio and Music Store at your service."

"This is Rillingham's Television and Music Shop at your service," Patty said in a high, sugary voice.

"Store, not shop," said Mr Rillingham, but without impatience. "And you left out 'Radio'. Let's start again. This is Rillingham's..."

She fluted each phrase after him until they had arrived at the formula, inviting the customer to name his wishes, in so far as they concerned Radio, Television or Music, and assuring him that they should be attended to as soon as the shop re-opened.

"Now, got that, Patty?" Mr Rillingham asked anxiously.

She nodded. "This is Rillingham's – "

"All right, all right," said Mr Rillingham. "I know you've got it. You're a clever girl. Now, what do we need to do to start the thing going? I suppose the telephone bell has to ring. Sidney, nip round to the box and – "

"No need, guv," said Mr Mayhew's man. "Fix it without. Tell me when you want it, thassall."

Mr Mayhew and Mr Rillingham joked a little together, about what a wonderful thing progress was, and then Mr Rillingham gave the signal, the man started the tape, and Patty spoke the message in a voice quite different from the one she had used in repeating it after Mr Rillingham. She dropped her voice almost an octave and gave it an American intonation, saying "Rilling-ham" instead of the English "Rillingham." When she had finished, Sidney half expected someone to comment on the difference, but no one did.

Patty's face had assumed a bright smile as she addressed the instrument, as is usual among people of primitive mental organi-sation, and she now kept this smile firmly in place, looking from Mr Rillingham to Mr Mayhew, and even fleetingly at Sidney, then back to Mr Rillingham.

"Well done, all," said Mr Rillingham. "Did you get the way it works, Sidney?"

"Dead simple, reely," said Mr Mayhew's man, straightening up.

The middle-aged cafeteria owner now joined them, fleetingly, on his way to the door.

"Merry Christmas," he said savagely.

"Find what you wanted, sir?" Mr Rillingham asked affably. "My young lady's just coming to – "

"I can see she is," said the cafeteria owner. "Trouble is, I'm just going." He walked to the door. "Wish *I* could keep people waiting while I messed about," he said wistfully. "Go out of business if I did." He went out and shut the door.

"I like that!" Mr Rillingham clucked. "Wasn't waiting five minutes!"

"Seven, actually," said Sidney. He knew before he spoke that it was a mistake to correct Mr Rillingham, but he felt aggressive all of a sudden.

"All right, all right, my lad," said Mr Rillingham with consid-erable petulance, "We all know *you've* got a good watch. *You're* always aware of the time, I've no doubt."

"Like some of mine," Mr Mayhew put in, staring at Sidney and nodding his head sympathetically. "If they don't know any-thing else they know what time it is."

Mr Mayhew's man, standing behind his employer, winked at

Sidney. But this failed to put Sidney into a good temper. He felt himself blushing hotly. No doubt he would have burst out with some hot retort to Mr Rillingham, but the number of retorts he felt like making was so large that they became confused and nothing came out. He wanted to call Mr Rillingham a fat-arsed old clot and also a crafty old shark. He wanted to shout, for the whole shop to hear, that Patty was a phony with her artificial voice and her ninety photographs of Elvis the Pelvis and that she wouldn't live a day in the business only for her vital statistics. He wanted to tell Mr Mayhew to go and sew his big mouth up with fuse wire. Consequently, he said nothing, but stood there and flushed and glared. Mr Mayhew's man winked again and this time shrugged as well. He was good-natured, in his taciturn way, Sidney could tell.

"Well, back to work before we lose any more trade," said Mr Rillingham in a heavy voice, from which a great deal of the geniality had drained away. He looked accusingly at Sidney as if *he* were the one who was losing trade.

It was now about three o'clock, and Sidney had some orders to deliver before nightfall. He loaded the orders into the van and drove off. Driving the van was one of the things he liked best about the job; he drove skilfully and fast, and as he wove in and out of the traffic his spirits revived. After all, he reflected, he had it pretty good. A radio and TV serviceman was safe for life. It was the job of the present and the job of the future, too. The van hummed along, growling in low gear through traffic, skimming over the clear patches in top like a bird, and Sidney felt better every minute.

He delivered a few sets, adapted a few plugs, accepted cups of tea and, in one hospitable house, a slice of Christmas cake. Then, towards five, came his last call. New tube for a television set in a big, comfortable-looking Georgian house.

"Class," said Sidney to himself as he rang the bell.

He waited. It was cold, and he was just about to ring again when the door opened. Inside stood a beautiful fair-haired girl. A real smashing piece of crumpet, Sidney thought. He wondered for an instant if he was dreaming; but the comfortable solidity and bulk of his bag of tools and the spare parts in a bundle under his arm reassured him that this was happening.

"Rillingham's," he said, with an impressive air. The girl just stood and looked puzzled, so he added, "Mend the television."

The girl brightened. "Oh, tallivishn!" she said. Her voice was better than Patty's: light, but not so thin. "Comm in, wun't you?"

"Won't I just," Sidney thought. He stepped inside, careful to keep his feet on the mat, and shut the door behind him. "Where's the set?" he asked.

The girl led him down a corridor and through a door at the far end. It was full of toys and children's garments. The furniture was of plain wood, scrubbed white, and there were brightly coloured pictures tacked to the walls.

"Kid's room, eh?" said Sidney brightly. "What they got, *two* TV sets?" For there, in the middle of the room, stood the set he was required to mend. Its polished, veneered wood looked odd against the self-conscious plainness of the other fittings.

The girl told him no, only one. It was kept in the nursery because her employers were not interested in television and thought it was mostly for children. But she was interested in it. She was the *au pair* girl. Sidney did not know what "oh pear" meant, but he gathered that she mainly looked after the children and that she had three hours off every day. Normally she went out in her three hours but this afternoon her employers had taken the children out and the house was so nice and quiet that she thought she would stay in, especially as she knew the television set was going to be mended and she had been missing it. She added that she was from Switzerland.

Sidney, working mechanically, had by this time got the entrails of the television set out on the floor. He could see at once a dozen ways in which this could be turned into a long job. But *long*. He could telephone Mr Rillingham and say he wouldn't back until after closing time and they might as well close the shop without him; he would garage the van.

He stole a glance at the girl. She must like him, or at any rate not *not* like him, if she was prepared to loaf about talking to him in her funny English while he repaired the set. And she was foreign. She might be lonely. Of course, she had class, but foreign class didn't count, and anyway who was better than a TV and radio technician these days? It was the *future* that counted. In a flash, Sidney saw himself driving about, not in a van but in a chromium-heavy saloon car, with the beautiful Swiss girl sitting beside him and a fat cigar in his mouth. The future, the future!

The Swiss girl met Sidney's eyes as he glanced up at her, and gave him a delicious smile.

"You like to do that?" she asked, nodding towards the scatter of television entrails. Sidney was startled at first, then realised that she was asking him whether he was happy in his work. It was just the opening he wanted.

"I'll say I like it," he said. "Best work in the world. Radio and TV maintenance. Work of the future. Mind you, it's crowded."

"Yes,?" said the girl. She gave him her delicious smile again.

"But *crowded*," said Sidney. "Everybody wants to get into it. But ninety per cent don't get further than – well, the ruddyments. Wiring and installation."

He looked up at the girl to see if she was with him, and she said "Yes?" again.

"No brains, see," Sidney explained. "It's no mug's game, messing with these babies." He smiled affectionately down at the television set. "Even me, I know a pretty fair amount, I've worked with most types – and I'll admit, straightaway, there's things about radio and TV that *I* don't know."

"Yes?"

"I don't know *yet*, I should say. But I will. I go to evening classes down at the Tek. That's what we call the Technical College. I aim to know it all backwards – theory and practice. *Backwards*. Got most of it at my finger-tips now. Because you know what? I'm moving, I'm going places."

He stood up, and found that his eyes were just on a level with the girl's. She was tall. He liked that.

She smiled again, not seeming at all nervous, and said, "You are an angineer?"

Sidney smiled. He liked the way she talked, and he even liked the way she sometimes pronounced "e" as "a".

"Engineer? Yes, in a way," he said. "But I'm not staying on the engineering side all my life. I'll just master it thoroughly and then I'll get over on to the executive side. There's a place waiting for me any time I care to say, only I'm taking my time. Mr Rillingham, that's my boss, he'd take me into the management side any time I asked him. At the moment I'm, well, what you might call the chief executive organiser of the servicing department. It's a big firm, y'know, Rillingham's. Very big way of business."

"Yes?"

"Very very big," said Sidney. "And developing all the time. Of course, I'm only a junior partner, as yet. But everyone has to start some time. That's what Mr Rillingham said when he gave me my partnership. 'It's only a junior one for the time being, Sidney,' he said. 'But say the word when you're ready – in your own time, mind – to come into the executive side, and we'll start grooming you for an equal partnership with me. Split the business fifty-fifty.' As he talked, Sidney had a vision of Mr Rillingham, standing in front of a mammoth factory, waving a plump hand towards it. Cars and wagons were moving in and out of the picture in the background, and Mr Rillingham, smiling, held out a document with a blob of red sealing-wax in the corner.

"I have saw, have *seen*, your shop," said the Swiss girl. "On the corner from Rampart Road."

"*One* of our shops," Sidney corrected her. "As a matter of fact, that little old shop you saw is just kept on for interest reasons, see: sentimental, and all that. It was the original one, where the first Mr Rillingham started the business, way back." He felt pleased with that touch. "The *first* Mr Rillingham" was good. "It's a big chain, now: shops all over. And up-to-date! You never saw anything like it. Equipment! Cor!"

Seized by a sudden idea, he looked at his watch. "Listen, to show you how up-to-date we are," he said. "The shop'll be shut in ten minutes or so. Let's wait, give 'em time, and then you put a call through."

"Put a – "

"Go on, just to please me," he grinned. "I won't tell you, else it'd spoil the surprise. But if you telephone our place after shop-closing time, I guarantee you quite a surprise."

The next half-hour passed quickly. Sidney put through a quick call and told Patty, who answered, that he was held up on a telly servicing job and wouldn't be back until after the shop closed. He would put the van away and see them again the day after Boxing Day. He hung up quickly, before she could bring up any objection to this, and went to work on the television set. The job was, in fact, not a very long one, and he had everything neatly cleared up within the half-hour.

"Now," he said, glancing at his watch. "That should've given them time to finish up and get clear, even if it *is* Christmas Eve, so let's put through that call."

"Does it work now?" the girl asked.

"Yes, yes," said Sidney. He turned knobs, to reassure her, and a picture flashed on to the screen.

"Oh!" cried the girl. "It's Mel Chain! He is my best actor!"

"Okay, okay," said Sidney, feeling irritation welling up again. "Never mind for a moment: You've got all night to watch Mel – "

"I'm coming," said the girl. Contrite, she flashed him her smile.

Together they walked down the corridor. Sidney realised that this was the greatest moment of his life. This girl made Patty look like the big phony she was. Her vital statistics might not be quite so striking, on paper, but Sidney knew that there was a lot to this business that never got on to paper.

He told the girl what number to dial, and stood by with a confident smile to watch her reaction. While he waited, he felt suddenly very fond of Rillingham's, as an idea, and even quite fond, or at least tolerant, of Mr Rillingham. Even Patty, within her phony limits, was probably not a bad sort of girl.

Patty, Mr Rillingham. In the silence of the house, he could hear the telephone ringing at the other end.

"What goes on?" he demanded. There was a queer sinking sensation in his inside.

The girl smiled at him, just the same as before, but in the colder atmosphere of the entrance hall it seemed to him that her smile was mechanical, something she could just flash on and off.

"Give," he said brusquely, and took the receiver from her. It was getting the ringing tone, right enough. What went on? Had Mr Rillingham, fool that he was, locked up the shop and gone out without setting the answering device? Surely he would never – . But if there had been anyone in the shop, they would have answered it by now. Fools! They were gone, and the brilliant new device was not even in use. What was the good of – .

He stopped. Someone had picked up the receiver.

"Yes? Who is it?"

The voice of Mr Rillingham, sounding annoyed and rather flustered.

Sidney opened his mouth, then closed it again. No good giving himself away.

"This is Rillingham's Radio and TV Service," Mr Rillingham barked. "We're closed. It's way after closing time and we're closed. Was there something important...hello? hello? HELLO!"

His voice was so full anger that Sidney felt quite scared, even though he knew he was perfectly safe. He hung up quickly and looked round for the girl.

"It seems there's a slight technical – oh," he trailed off. The girl was opening the front door and a crowd of people were coming in. Mother, father, kids, dogs, parcels. The girl was chattering away to the parents in a foreign language, the children were shrieking in English, and a small dog began to bark joyously.

"Oh, Crippen. Oh, stone the bleeding crows," Sidney said to the silent telephone.

Observed by no one, he picked up his bag of tools and went out through the door. Then he got into the van and drove back to the shop through the Christmas traffic. Every time he stopped at the lights, he thought of Mr Rillingham and Patty in the darkened, locked-up shop.

There were six traffic-lights in all, and by the time he got back to the shop Sidney had had all he could take. He drove the van into its garage down the street, locked the garage, walked to the shop, let himself in with the key Mr Rillingham didn't know he had had made (just because it irked him to be without a key) and strode noisily down between the counters. He did not snap on the lights because he hoped to catch Mr Rillingham and Patty lying behind one of the counters, or wedged behind Mr Rillingham's desk.

There was nothing. They had gone, of course. He could just hear Mr Rillingham saying to Patty, "Come on: let's get out of here before some other blinking deaf mute rings up," and the pair of them getting into Mr Rillingham's car, slamming the doors and gliding off, just as he had seen himself gliding with the Swiss girl.

Out of curiosity, he switched a light on and went over to look at the telephone-answering apparatus. Yes, Mr Rillingham had left it correctly coupled to the instrument. That must have been his last action before going out and locking the door.

"An unsleeping secretary," said Sidney. "Big White Deal." He uncoupled the apparatus and started the tape running. It repeated Patty's message, complete with deep tones and transatlantic intonation. Sidney reversed the machine and erased the message. Then he held the microphone to his mouth and said, "This is Rillingham's Television, Radio and Music Shop. A Merry Christmas to all our customers. We regret to announce that we shall be going out of business as of even date. It was a good business but we killed it with our inefficiency. Good-bye for ever. It has been a pleasure to serve you."

When he had recorded his message, Sidney coupled the apparatus to the telephone in the correct manner, switched off the light and left the shop. As he walked down the street he thought how glad he was that tomorrow was Christmas. He had been working too hard lately. Now he could take a rest, and there was no need to worry about finding another job because, quite soon, he would be doing his National Service.

Rafferty

He kept trying to take her arm, as they walked home from the cinema on that sweltering summer night. Her home, not his or theirs. He was seeing her home.

"Oh, Walter, *don't*," she said at last.

"But, darling – "

"No, *please* don't," she said.

He walked a few paces in silence, then exploded. "Well – how much longer is this going on?"

"Only till I feel sure."

"One way or another?"

He groaned, "But that might be ages."

"Walter, I've told you it won't be for ages. All I'm asking for is a little time. You asked me to marry you the third time you took me out – "

"Eleven days after I first saw you," he said tonelessly.

"Yes, and you know the state I was in."

The street was empty; there was no one to be startled by his sudden wild laugh.

"All right," she said, nettled. "I know you don't like to have it mentioned. But you might as well face facts."

"All right, I'll face facts. I'll face as many as you like. And I'd be happy if I thought you'd face one for every one *I* faced."

"Oh, don't be *silly*, please."

"Fact number one," he said loudly. "I met you when you'd just been chucked by Rafferty."

"Thanks for putting it so politely."

"Chucked. Thrown out. Pensioned off, only with no pension. Rafferty who'd played you along that he was going to marry you – "

"He never did that," she said quickly.

"All right, give him his due. He didn't actually *say* it. He just let you hope that if you went to bed with him and let him get used to you he'd feel he wanted you permanently about the place."

"You're wrong, you're so wrong. I always knew he wouldn't. He never does marry any of his girls."

"All right, by God, I'll give you *your* due. You wanted Rafferty so much you didn't care what happened or how long it lasted."

"I was in love with him. I don't see the point of denying that. But it's you who keep bringing it up, not me."

"Yes, it's I who keep bringing it up – for what *that's* worth."

"I've told you I don't see the point of denying it."

"I'm not asking you to deny it. You were in love with Rafferty and after he ditched you the world came to an end. It had just about sunk in that it *had* come to an end, that he *wasn't* going to take you back, when you met me."

"And eleven days later you proposed to me," she said. They turned into the street where she lived. The refined moon of Kensington shone down gently, the hum of the traffic was muffled by the jumble of narrow lanes.

"I proposed to you. And three months have gone by."

"Three *months!*" she said, stopping. "And do you realise that if we got married we'd be together for about forty-five *years?*"

"Yes," he said. "Yes, I realise it."

"Well, then."

"But, Isobel, listen to me. . . ." They were walking on. "It isn't a question of time – not as much as you make it, anyway. Just because marriage is for a long time, it doesn't mean that you've got to know somebody for a long time to get to know them."

"Doesn't it?"

"Of course not. I knew I wanted to marry you as soon as ever I met you."

"Yes," she said slowly, "but you weren't. . ."

"No, I wasn't just on the rebound from a terrific love affair where I'd been whirled up to the heights and then had my heart broken."

"I never said my heart was broken."

"No. All right. You never said it."

They had reached the door of her flat, and she opened her handbag to look for the key.

"Isobel – for God's sake – "

"Well, yes, Walter," she said calmly. "Since you've mentioned *rebound*, we might as well be frank. I *was* on the rebound."

"Was? You mean you *are*, don't you?"

"You needn't be so bitter. I've quite made my mind up to it that everything's over between me and. . .that it's all finished – "

"Between you and Rafferty," he said viciously. "Why don't you say it? Are you frightened of a name? Rafferty, Rafferty,

Rafferty! There, perhaps that'll exorcise it."

"I wish you'd control yourself," she said, still calmly. "As I say, I've buried the past. Only – "

"Only you're afraid it'll come rearing up out of its grave and claim you again. It shouldn't have any difficulty in shaking off the depth of earth *you've* been able to put over it. About half an inch, I should say."

"All I'm asking, and I don't know how many times you want me to say it, is that I need a little breathing space. I've seen what happens to girls who marry on the rebound. I've told you that I'm considering your proposal – "

"And how much longer are you going to go on considering it, for God's sake?"

"I want to keep it in mind while I get to know you better."

"Well, look – if you want to get to know me better, why don't – "

"Oh, no," she said wearily, "Not *that* again. I tell you absolutely once and for all that I refuse to have all *that* again."

He was silent, letting his hands fall to his sides.

"Well, look," she said more gently. "I'm tired and I shall go in now and go to bed. Thank you for taking me out, Walter."

"Marry me," he said.

"Don't fret," she said, still gently. "I'm doing all I can about it. After all, I'm not trifling with you, am I?"

"Not like you trifled with Rafferty," he said.

In an instant the key was out, it was inserted and twisted, the door opened and she was stepping inside.

"Isobel . . . no, please. . . . "

"Good night."

"But, please, darling, just a second. . . . I'm sorry. I'm just as angry with myself as you could possibly be with me."

"I can believe that."

"Please, darling – it just slipped out before I knew what I was saying – I didn't mean to – "

"*Didn't mean to!*" she hissed. "Why don't you admit you're so absolutely mad with jealousy that you can't keep off the topic – you have to keep picking at it like a scab, a disgusting scab?"

"Oh, God, Isobel, I can't *help* it. . . . It's true I can't keep off the subject, but who could if they were in my situation? Look, darling – you've been in love, surely you can see. . . . You must know what it's like. Weren't you ever jealous yourself?"

"Jealous?" she said, with a new edge in her voice. "What girl ever loved *him* and escaped being made jealous?"

"Well, then...."

"But I had more control over my feelings than to make an exhibition of myself."

"Make an exhibition of yourself," he repeated sadly. "How *English* you are.... You think the important thing to do about feelings is to hide them, don't you? But remember this: if you had more success in concealing your jealousy than I have, after all you were getting *some* consolation – your affair with Rafferty wasn't just one long series of bangs against a brick wall like mine with you."

"Consolation?" she asked wonderingly.

"You were sleeping with him, to put it bluntly."

"Good night." She was inside and the door was closing.

"Isobel – let me ring you – "

The door was held open long enough for him to hear, "I've made myself perfectly clear on that point. I do *not* want you ringing me up all the time. I've told you that I shall ring you when I've any suggestion to make about going out, and I mean what I say. If you ring me just once more, if I pick up the receiver and hear that it's you, I'll just ring off and that will be the last we'll ever have to do with each other. Is that clear?"

"Yes," he said softly.

"Then good night, Walter."

"Good night. Western 8864."

"I've got it, you know that," she said, and the door closed.

"Walter?"

"Isobel – is that really you?"

"Who else?"

"I've been waiting by the telephone every night."

"Well, don't sound so sorry for yourself. It was last Wednesday we went to the cinema, so that only makes five nights."

"*Only!*"

"Well, cheer up. I've got good news for you. We're going to a party."

"Oh."

"You don't sound pleased."

"Will it be a party at which I shall have the slightest chance of getting you alone for a few minutes?"

"That will depend on how you behave."

"I thought you wanted to get to know me."

" So I do, but one can learn a lot about a person by seeing how they behave in company with other people."

"What kind of people will they be?"

"I'm not sure; the kind you won't like, probably. Smart people. It's one of Roderick and Helen's parties."

"Will *you* like them?"

"I might. Anyway, I want to go. Call for me to-morrow evening? I think it starts about nine."

"Will you come out to dinner first?"

"Thanks, I'd love to."

"I'll come at half past seven, then."

"No, eight. I shan't be ready by half past seven."

They went on talking for a few minutes, without his succeeding in negotiating a more generous allowance of her time.

After an hour at the party, Walter felt ready to congratulate himself. Apart from a perfunctory word of greeting from their host and hostess, no one had spoken to them. The guests all seemed to know each other very well, and to be in any case too supercilious and unpleasant to address a word to anyone they did not know. As a result, he had been able to steer Isobel into a corner and hold her attention without any difficulty. It was true that she kept glancing over his shoulder to see if there were any prospect of better entertainment; but he had never expected things to be perfect, and was quite happy to settle for them as they were.

So the first hour ticked by pleasantly. But the second was not many minutes old when it happened.

"Isobel, keep still." He was looking over her shoulder towards the door. "Don't turn round."

"Why on earth not?"

"I mean just prepare yourself for a bit of a shock before you turn round."

"Whatever...? You're talking as if a ghost had come in."

He did not answer.

"Walter – is it – "

"It's Rafferty," he said. "He's just come in and he's talking to Roderick and Helen."

"I didn't know he knew them," she whispered.

They stood perfectly still for a moment. Then, with an abrupt gesture, she moved aside and put down her empty glass. At the same time she turned so that her profile would be visible from the doorway.

"Thanks for telling me, Walter," she said in a firm voice. "And now there's no need to refer to it any more. Thanks to you I shan't find myself coming face to face with him out of the blue...and that was the only thing that would have upset me. As long as I know he's here and I can keep a look out, it makes no difference at all."

"He's with a girl," said Walter, staring hard without giving the impression of doing so.

"You needn't tell me that. He's always with one."

"I'd say he'd picked rather a winner this time."

"All right, you needn't go on about it."

"I'm not going on about it. I'm just saying he's picked a winner. Chestnut hair framing an absolutely poignant little heart-shaped face."

"Thank you. I'll turn round in due course and see her for myself."

"And very big eyes."

"*Thank* you, Walter. My own eyes may not be very big, but they're big enough to see a girl's face across a room, so you needn't keep filling in details about this one." Her voice had sharpened.

"You're upset," he said, eyeing her considerately. "It's upset you, naturally, his suddenly turning up. Shall we go?"

"Of course not."

"I could easily tell Roderick and Helen that we've got an inescapable engagement for later on."

"You won't do anything of the kind. Why am I to be driven away from a party, even a not very enjoyable one, just because this wretched man turns up? Why, he might turn up anywhere I go for the rest of my life."

"And always with a different girl."

"As you tactfully say, always with a different girl."

"Though I wouldn't blame him if he stuck to this one. She's a winner."

"Walter, if you tell me she's a winner again I promise you faithfully I shall scream."

"But she is a winner," he said mutinously.

"I promise you *faithfully* I shall scream the *place* down if you say one more thing about her."

"No, you won't. If you screamed, everybody would think you were having an emotional crisis because Rafferty's walked in."

"Of course they wouldn't," she said hotly. "I don't suppose there's a single person here who knows anything about it."

He laughed shortly. "That's good. You know what Rafferty does when he's not actually making love, don't you? He sits in bars talking about it to anyone who'll listen."

"God, aren't you disgusting," she said, looking at him closely as if for the first time. "That awful jealousy that you're so eaten up with – it makes you so ugly."

"You don't think I'm not telling the truth, do you?"

"I don't care whether you're telling the truth or not. It's just so ugly, that's all. You're so absolutely insane with jealousy of him."

"Well, I will say this for him," said Walter. "He certainly does know how to pick them."

"You're not *still* harping on this wretched girl?"

"Not necessarily. After all, he picked you."

"Thank you for lumping us together."

Walter paused for a second before allowing himself the answer. "Well, if Rafferty lumped you together, I don't see why I shouldn't."

She slapped his face. In the mounting volume of noise from the party, the sound did not carry, and only a few people standing nearest them noticed and talked all the harder to insist that they had seen nothing.

"Well, what are you waiting for?" she hissed, her face scarlet and eyes brimming. "Go and start chasing this poignant heart-shaped little bitch. You've been trying hard enough to follow in his footsteps with me – why not start trying with her?"

"Perhaps he'll marry this one," Walter said flatly.

"Well, don't let that worry you. If he does, he'll soon be leaving her alone while he dates up half-a-dozen new ones at once. Make a nice role for you, wouldn't it? Consoler of the grief-stricken little heart-shaped big-eyes."

"Don't forget about the chestnut hair."

She whirled round and stared directly over to where Rafferty and the girl stood. For a full minute she stared with her eyes boring into the girl, never once swerving aside to look at Rafferty. In the end, under the pressure of concentration, the girl looked up, met the stare and said something to Rafferty, causing him to turn his big, handsome Irish head in their direction. He said something in reply, the girl smiled and they both turned away.

"There, now I've done it, haven't I?" Isobel rounded on Walter. "I've gone and made her turn her back to us. So now you can't stare at her face any more. Ruined your party, I expect – I'm *sorry*."

"Don't give it a thought. I'm enjoying the party all right. And anyway the back view looks all right, too."

"Do you want another slap?"

"Considering that slap was the first sign you've ever given of taking any real notice of me, I wouldn't mind."

She stood tensely still for a moment, then relaxed slowly, and a more gentle expression spread over her face.

"I see," she said in a low voice, laying her hand for an instant on his. "Sorry I was stupid." She looked at him almost tenderly. "But you don't really have to, you know, Walter."

"Have to what?"

"Make me jealous." She smiled. "Come on, admit that's what you were doing."

"Well," he said, looking away, "jealousy is a horrible feeling."

She smiled indulgently. "It was stupid of me not to have understood sooner."

"Shall we circulate a bit?" he said. "Otherwise we'll find it's time to go home and we shan't have spoken to a soul."

"We'll have spoken to each other."

"Yes, but still, we have a duty toward the party."

She shrugged, and they began to move round the room. Walter filled Isobel's glass, and turned back to the table to fill his own. While she was momentarily alone, a girl she knew slightly spoke to her and drew her into conversation with a knot of people whose names, thrown at her abruptly, she hardly made any effort to catch.

Walter, his recharged glass in his hand, stood by the table, making no attempt to join Isobel. His eyes wandered about the room till they found Rafferty's girl. She really was a winner. Her neck was really like alabaster. He had not noticed her neck before, but now he was inclined to rate it as high as her heart-shaped face, big eyes and the very elegantly cut chestnut hair.

"That Rafferty knows how to pick them," he muttered.

Then Isobel was by his side. "Walter, I'm going to let you take me home."

"Are you?" he said.

"Yes, dear. I'm tired and I've had enough of the party. I won't ask you if *you've* had enough," she gave him a tenderly conspiratorial smile, "because you're always intriguing to avoid company and get me in a *tête-à-tête* . . . Well, here's your chance."

He fetched her coat, they murmured excuses and adieus, and the warm, still summer night received them.

"You know," she began, after they had walked in silence for some minutes, "in a way I'm not sorry that he turned up."

"No?"

"No! In fact, I'm quite glad."

So am I, he thought.

"It made everything a lot clearer to me," she went on.

Quite possibly Roderick knows who that girl is and where she lives, he thought.

"I mean, if you'd told me before I went that he was going to be there, I'd probably have felt so nervous I wouldn't have wanted to go. But there it was, I went, and he *was* there, and after all it didn't matter."

"No, it didn't," he said.

"It really brought home to me," said Isobel, "how *dead* all that is. I mean, my feelings for him. Absolutely *dead.*"

"Good thing," he said.

She was silent while they turned into the street where she lived. Then she said, "Is that all you've got to say?"

"Is what all?"

"Just that it's a good thing?"

He considered. "Well, it is a good thing, isn't it?"

They had reached her flat. "I don't think I'll ask you in, Walter," she said, opening her bag for the key. "I'm tired and I don't think I'd be very good company."

"You never have asked me in. Why should you start now?"

"No, that's right, why should I?" she said brightly.

The door was open. Inside was her empty flat. From where she stood on the pavement she could see her two overcoats hanging on pegs in the hall.

"Well, good night, Walter."

"Good night," he said. She moved hesitantly on to the doorstep as he began to walk away along the silent street. "Ring me sometime, won't you?" he said over his shoulder.

"When?"

"Oh, just any time. Just unexpectedly, as you did this time."

"Yes," she said, half speaking to herself, "unexpected things do rather appeal to you, don't they?"

She thought her voice probably too quiet to carry as far as where he stood, but he answered at once, in a polite conversational tone. "So they do; but, then, life's so full of unexpected things, it pays to cultivate a taste for them." He started to move away and added, "Well, good night, Isobel."

She stood watching him. Before reaching the corner, he turned and waved, though without interrupting his regular footfall.

"Thanks for taking me to the party," he called. "It was fun."

He turned the corner. She went into her empty flat and shut the door behind her. "It was fun, it was fun, it was fun," she said to the coats hanging up on their pegs.

The Valentine Generation

Quarter to eight on a Monday morning, well into April but still pretty fresh, and I'm off to a fair start with the collecting. I may be getting on towards retiring age, but I can still get round the boxes as quick as any of them and quicker than most. The secret is to get a move on in the early stages. Get round as many as you can by nine o'clock. After that, the traffic sets in heavy and slows you down so much that you can pretty well reckon to take double time over everything.

This morning I've got one of the light vans and it looks as if I'm getting away easy. I'm round the South-West Fifteen area, the other side of the river. Nice quiet surburban streets, with trees in fresh bloom. Like a trip to the country. So of course I let myself be lulled into feeling optimistic. Forty years with the Post Office and I *still* haven't got it into my head that trouble always hits you when you've got your guard down.

I'm coming up to the third box and even as I drive up to it I can see this girl standing there on the pavement. She's only a couple of yards away from the pillar-box, but my early warning system still doesn't go off: I think perhaps she's waiting for somebody to come out of one of the houses, some girl-friend she travels to work with or her little brother that she's seeing to school. Funny joke.

I get out of the van and go over to the box with my bunch of keys and my bag at the ready. And straight away I see that she's watching me. I try to take no notice, but her eyes are boring two holes in the back of my neck.

I open the box and there are the letters. Not many, because most people who post on a Sunday manage to catch the five-o'clock collection. About a couple of dozen in all. I'm just sweeping them into the bag when the girl takes a step towards me. I see her out of the corner of my eye and I straighten up. For a moment I wonder if I'm going to be coshed or something. There's a kind of desperation about her. But she's alone, a nice-looking girl, about twenty, good class, well dressed. She's very unhappy, I can see that. All stirred up about something. But it's no business of mine. On the collecting, you've no time to spare before nine o'clock. After that, you might just as well slacken off, that's what I always tell them.

I turn to go back to the van, but she's speaking to me. I don't quite catch what she's saying. She's too confused, the sounds just tumble out over one another.

"Anything wrong, Miss?" I say to her, but as I speak I'm opening the van door. She's not going to hold me up, whatever she wants.

"Yes," she says. "There's something terribly wrong. But you could put it right for me in a minute, if you'd be very kind."

I don't like the sound of that, but she's waiting for me to say something, so I decide to give her one minute of my time. Just one minute. She's in trouble, and I've got daughters of my own.

"What is it I can do for you?" I say. "It'd better be something I can do within sixty seconds, because on this job, it's all a question of how much you can do before nine – "

She doesn't let me finish. She's all over me, reaching out as if she wants to grab hold of my arm. "You can, you can easily do it straight away," she says. "It's just that – I've posted a letter that I ought never to have posted. And I want to get it back. If it goes it'll do terrible harm that I could never do anything about. You will give it me, won't you? Please?"

It's a funny thing, but as I stand there listening to her I have a kind of "This-is-where-I-came-in" feeling. All those years ago, when I first joined the Post Office, I used to wonder if anybody would ever come up to me when I was on collecting and ask me if they could have a letter back. And now at last it's happened. Of course I've always known I couldn't do it.

"Sorry, miss," I say, shaking my head. "Firmest rule in the book. Once a thing's posted, it's in the care of the Post Office until it reaches the party it's addressed to."

She draws a deep breath and I can see she's getting ready to work hard. "Look," she begins. But I'm too quick for her. "No, you look," I say to her. "Forty years I've worked for the Post Office, and all through those forty years it's been my living. A job to do, a wage, pension at the end of it, social club, met most of my friends through it one way and another. It's like being married. Forty years and you don't even want a change. You find you can't even imagine it any more."

"Being married!" she says, gulping, as if I'd said something that really hurt her. "I wouldn't know. I've never been married yet, and if you're going to stand on those regulations of yours and refuse to give just one little letter back, just *once* in forty years, I don't suppose I ever shall be."

It's not that I'm heartless, but at that I just have to laugh. "Oh, come *on*," I say to her. "A pretty young thing like you. Never married, that's a laugh!"

"Oh, you're so clever," she says, sad and angry at the same time. "You know everything, don't you? All right, probably if my entire happiness is ruined, I'll get over it one day, enough to marry somebody just for the sake of having a normal life and a family. But I shan't be happy."

"We've all had it," I say. "Nobody in the world's good enough except just one person."

"Don't you believe in love?" she asks.

"Well, as a matter of fact I do," I say. "I got married myself, soon after I joined the Post Office, and I can't believe I'd have been so happy with anyone else as I have with my wife. I did all right when I picked her out. But that was back in the days when marriages were made to last. Everything's different with you young people today."

"You think so?" she says. "Really different?"

"Course it is," I say. "All the romance has gone out of it. Well, look at it. Sex, sex, sex from morning to night and never a bit of sentiment."

"What's wrong with sex?" she says, looking stubborn.

"Nothing," I say, "only in my day we didn't try to build a fire with nothing but kindling."

I turn away, thinking I'll leave her to chew that one over. I'm just getting the van door open when suddenly she's there, grabbing at my wrist.

"Please," she says. "*Please.* You've got a kind face. I know you'd help me if only you knew."

"Well, I haven't got time to know," I say, trying to get free. "I thought you said it would be sixty seconds."

"I wrote a letter to the man I'm in love with," she says, speaking very quickly and holding on to my wrist. "A horrible, hurtful letter telling him I didn't want any more to do with him, and saying a lot of horrible things that weren't even true. Things I just made up to try to hurt him – to make him suffer."

"And now you're sorry for him," I say. "Well, write him another letter and tell him it was all a pack of lies."

"You don't understand," she says. "It isn't that I'm sorry for him, it's just that I want him back. And he'll never, *never* come back to me if he reads that letter. He'll never forgive me."

"He will if he loves you," I say.

"Oh, it's hopeless," she says with a kind of groan. "You talk as if love was so simple."

"Well, so it is," I tell her. "If two people love each other, they want to be nice, and help each other, and make things easy. I know there are lovers' quarrels, but they're soon patched up. Why, that's all part of the fun of being in love. You'll find out when the real thing comes along."

"The real thing!" she groans again. "I tell you this is the real thing, all the way through. Look, why don't you believe me and let me take my letter back?"

"I've told you why," I say. "Forty years with the Post Office and you want me to start ignoring regulations?"

"All right," she says, speaking very low and looking at me fiercely. "Go ahead and keep your regulations. But think about it sometimes in the middle of the night. How you sacrificed somebody's happiness for the whole of their life, rather than break a regulation."

"I've told you before, you're being silly," I say. "Look, I'll prove it to you. Number one, you don't really love this bloke."

"Don't love him!" she wails. "How can you possibly tell that?"

"Well, does it look like it?" I say. "You get your rag out about something, and straight away you write him such a stinking letter, full of insults and things that aren't even true, that you daren't go near him once he reads it."

"That doesn't prove I don't love him," she says. "All it proves is that I was desperate. Look, let me tell you what happened."

"All right," I say, "but make it fast. And don't kid yourself that I'll give you the letter when you've finished." I meant it, too. Regulations mean a lot after forty years.

"I usually spend Saturday evening with Jocelyn," she begins. *Jocelyn.* I don't like the sound of that. "And last Saturday, that's the day before yesterday, he rings up and tells me he can't do it. He's got to look after his aunt who's coming up from the country. So when my brother and sister-in-law happened to look in and see me, I said I'd go out with them for the evening. We went up to the West End and I said I'd show them a nice little restaurant I know. So we went into this place and the very first person I saw was Jocelyn."

"With his aunt from the country," I say.

"With his aunt from the country," she says, nodding and looking very grim. "About twenty years old with a lot of red hair and a dress cut very low. And there was Jocelyn, leaning towards her the way he does when he's really interested in a girl."

"What a surprise for him," I say.

"No surprise," she says. "He never saw me. I knew at once I wouldn't be able to stand it. I wasn't going to have a show-down with him there and then, and as for sitting down and watching the performance and trying to eat my dinner, with my brother and his wife there on top of everything else, well."

"So you ducked out quick, and came home and wrote him a nasty letter," I say. Nine o'clock's creeping up and I'm ruddy nowhere with my collecting.

"If only I could have come straight home," she says. "But I have my brother and his wife to cope with. He's always saying I can't look after myself. I wasn't going to talk about it to him. So I looked round quickly and said sorry, this was the wrong place and I'd made a mistake. They said it looked all right and they'd like to try it anyway, but I said no, I was so keen to show them this special place. So there we were, out in the street, with them waiting for me to guide them and me with no idea where to go. We wandered about for ages, and my brother was in a filthy temper, and then I took them into a place and pretended that was it and it was awful. Oh, it was all so utterly, utterly awful I couldn't even talk. I could only say yes and no when they seemed to expect me to say something. I expect they thought I was mad."

"So after *that* you wrote him a letter," I say, trying to move her along even though the collections have now gone for a dead Burton.

"After that," she says, "I go home and spend a completely sleepless night. I don't even close my eyes, because every time I close them I see Jocelyn's face as he leans towards this girl."

"All right, let him lean," I say. "If he's the type that runs after every bit of skirt he sees, he won't make you happy anyway."

"But he *does* make me happy," she says. "He's absolutely ideal for me. He makes me feel marvellous. When I'm with him I'm really glad about being a woman."

"Even if you can't trust him?" I ask.

"Casual infidelities don't matter," she says. "It's the really deep communication between a man and woman that matters."

I can see this is getting out of my league altogether, so I make one more effort to brush her off. "All right," I say. "If your Jocelyn is in the deep-communication business, he won't be put off by a nasty letter. He'll see straight away that you only wrote it because you were angry or desperate or whatever it is."

"You're wrong," she says, looking at me very steadily. "There are some insults a man can't forgive. Listen, I wrote that letter on Sunday afternoon. I'd been crying nearly all morning, and every time I sat down to write I was just crying too much to see the paper. By the time I got down to it I was feeling murderous. I wrote things that I knew he'd find absolutely unforgivable. I laughed at him, I told him he hadn't been adequate for me, that I'd had other lovers all the time we'd been together. I must have been mad. I wrote so many details he'll never believe it isn't true."

"You say you love him?" I ask.

"I love him and need him utterly," she says.

"Rubbish," I say. The whole thing is beginning to get me down. "If that's love, so is a boxing match. It's just vanity and sex, that's all it is. There's no love anywhere."

"Well, perhaps that's not a bad definition," she says, as if I've got all day to stand there and discuss it. "I mean, one's need for another person is partly vanity isn't it? It's all bound up with one's own belief in oneself."

"One this and one that," I say. "You're just hair-splitting. If you love anybody, you care for them, don't you? You want them to be happy."

"That's a chocolate-boxy idea of love," she says. "I mean it's not what happens when real people get involved with each other. You may have been able to live your life by those ideas, but in that case you've been very lucky. You've never had to face reality."

Reality! From a chit of a girl like this I'm learning about reality!

"Oh, I'm sure you've had lots of reality in your life," she says. "I know you've had all sorts of responsibilities and everything. It's just that your personal relationships must have been unreal. You wouldn't talk about love in that sort of Royal Doulton way if they hadn't been."

All at once I understood. She's not giving me her own opinions. She's just parroting what this Jocelyn's been teaching her. Deep communication between man and woman! I can just see his idea of it. Especially if he's got her trained so that she doesn't even count the other girls he runs after. And Royal Doulton! That's not the sort of thing she'd think up for herself.

"Listen to me, miss," I say. "Take an old man's advice and

leave that letter where it is. If it puts an end to this business between you and this Jocelyn bloke, believe me, you'll live to be grateful."

At that she stares at me as if she's caught me doing something so horrible she can't trust her own eyesight.

"It's unbelievable," she says at last. "If anybody had told me that – that ordinary human beings were capable of such stupidity and cruelty, yes, *cruelty*, I wouldn't have believed them." And she begins to cry, quite silently, with the tears running down her nose.

"Which of us is cruel?" I ask her. "Me, or Jocelyn?"

"You, of course," she says, so cross at what she thinks is cheek on my part that she stops crying. "You're making me miserable *for ever* just so that you won't have to admit that your ideas about love are out of date and wrong."

"Whereas Jocelyn is sweetness and kindness itself, eh?" I put in.

"No, of course not," she says. "He's capable of hardness and aggressiveness and he can be cruel himself at times. That's all part of his being a real man, the sort of man who can make a girl feel good about being feminine." That's another bit of Jocelyn's patter, if I'm any judge. "A man who was *sweetness and kindness itself*," she goes on, bringing out the words as if they're choking her, "wouldn't be capable of making a woman feel fulfilled and happy. He's got to have a streak of – of – "

"Of the jungle in him?" I say, trying to help her out.

"If you like, yes," she says, nodding and looking solemn.

"Well, I don't like," I say, letting it rip for once. "I think you're a nice girl, but you're being very silly. You've let this Jocelyn stuff your head full of silly ideas, you've taken his word for it that he can chase every bit of skirt he meets, tell lies to you, string you along every inch of the way, and it all doesn't matter because he's going to make you feel happy and relaxed, he's Tarzan of the flipping Apes. No, listen to me," I tell her, because I can see she's trying to stick her oar in, "I've stood here and listened to your story and made myself so late that the collections won't be right for the whole of today, and now I'm going to tell you what you ought to do. You're a nice girl. Cut this Jocelyn out of your life like the rotten thing he is. Go and find some young man who'll tell you that as a woman you deserve to be cherished and taken care of. Who'll love you enough to tell you the truth and play fair with you. Even if he isn't an animal out of the Zoo. Make do with an ordinary human being," I say to her. "You'll find it cheaper in the long run."

Instead of answering, she just stands there crying. All right, I think to myself, let her get on with it. I've given her the right advice and that's the end.

I get into the van and press the self-starter. I'd left the engine running but it doesn't idle fast enough on these crisp mornings, and it'd stalled. So anyway, I start it up and I'm just going to engage gear and move off when, for some reason, I can't do it. My foot comes off the accelerator and I look out of the window. There she is, still crying. Now's your cue to call me a sentimental old fool.

So I get out of the van again and I go back to where she's standing, crying her eyes out.

"Look, miss," I say, "it's the best thing, you know. He wouldn't have been any good to you."

"Why . . ." she begins, but she's crying too much to talk. I wait a bit and she has another go and this time it comes out. "Why are you so sure that you know best and that I must be wrong?" she asks me.

"Well, it's simple," I say. "I've had a happy marriage for nearly forty years. So naturally I know how they work. I know what you have to do."

"But love *changes*!" she says, bringing it out as if she's struggling for words that'll convince me. "I'm sure you've been happy, but you're wrong if you think that your way of being happy would work for young people of today. You belong to a different generation."

"And that makes me not human?" I ask. "Look, I've been happy with May for forty years and we've had three children. That's not done without love."

"Your kind of love," she says. "Your generation's kind. I'll bet you used to send each other Valentines with sentimental rhymes on them."

That gets my rag out. "Yes, so we damn well did," I say. "And not only that. We used to give one another keepsakes. Listen, the first time we ever went for a walk in the country, when we were courting, I picked some flowers for May and she took them home and pressed them between the leaves of a book – *and she's got them today*! Can you understand that? I wanted to love her and take care of her because she was a woman – that was the way I made her feel good, not telling her a lot of stuff about deep communication and keeping one eye out for the next little piece that came in sight. Valentines!" I say, and I must be speaking quite loud, because some people on the other side of the road stop and stare at me, "yes, we sent each other Valentines, big ones made of lace paper, shaped like hearts, some of 'em. That's something else you wouldn't understand. Try talking to Jocelyn about hearts!"

That's done it. I've got carried away and now I'm as upset as she is. I'm about ready to burst out crying myself. And me forty years with the Post Office. At this rate nobody'll get any letters at all.

"You think I don't know what love is, don't you?" the girl says. "You're quite sure that whatever I feel for Jocelyn, it's not love."

"Not what I'd call love," I tell her. "But you've got to excuse me. I don't know what love's supposed to be nowadays. I come from the wrong generation."

"The Valentine generation," she says and all of a sudden she's smiling at me, yes, *smiling*.

"Weren't there women in your generation," she says, "who loved men and went on loving them even if they didn't treat them right? Didn't they sometimes love husbands who got drunk or stayed away all night?"

"I've known the type," I say.

"And what did you think about them?" she goes on. "Did you think they were just fools who didn't know what they were doing?"

"That was different," I say. "A woman might go on loving a husband who mistreated her. But at least she didn't say that she loved him *because* he mistreated her. She loved him in *spite* of it."

"Are you sure?" she says. "Was it always as clear as that just why she loved him?"

"What are you getting at?" I ask.

"I'm trying to get you to admit," she says, "that other people might know what love is besides you."

"I'm quite sure they do," I say. "All I'm telling you is that you're wrong if you think you love this Jocelyn. You can't love a man who brings you so low."

"And you're not even going to let me try," she says, not crying now but just looking steadily into my face.

"Look," I say, just to finish it. "Let's have a bargain. You tell me what you think love is, and if I agree with you I'll give you your letter back."

"Just that?" she says. "Just tell what I think love is?"

"Yes," I say. I'm quite certain that whatever she says it'll be Jocelyn's angle.

"And you'll give me the letter back?" she says.

"If I agree with what you say, yes," I say.

"Well," she says, without even stopping to think, "it's – wanting to be with somebody all the time."

"All the time? You're sure?" I ask her.

"It's wanting to wake up with the same person every morning and do everything together and tell each other everything," she says.

"You know that, do you?" I say.

"Yes," she says. "I know that."

I go over to the van and get the bag out. If anybody sees this, I can be sacked, forty years or no forty years. But there's hardly anybody about, and a bargain's a bargain.

"I'll be very quick," she says, rummaging away. She shuffles the envelopes like a pack of cards and in no time at all she's found her letter and it's away, safe and sound, in her handbag.

"Bless you," she says. "I knew you'd want to help me really."

"I did want to help you," I say, "and I still think I'd have helped you more if I'd hung on to that letter."

"Don't worry about me," she says, smiling.

"Just tell me one thing," I say as I'm opening the van door. "Your idea of love. Would you say it was the same as Jocelyn's?"

"No," she says, as chirpy as a sparrow. "It's quite different."

"What's going to happen, then," I ask her, "if you've both got different ideas about love?"

"I'll take care of that," she says. I can see she's not worried at all. "It's what I feel for him that matters, not what he feels for me. I just want him around, that's all."

I get into the van and this time I drive away. The collections are up a big, tall gum tree. I have plenty of time stuck in traffic jams and I keep thinking of her and Jocelyn. How she doesn't care what he is or what he thinks or even what he *does*, so long as she has him. Doesn't sound like happiness to me. But all at once, the thought comes to me, well, she'll probably get what she wants. I mean to say, it didn't take her long to get me to break a Post Office regulation I'd never broken in forty years. She twisted me round her little finger, so it could be she'll twist him.

But then, of course, I'm soft-hearted compared with a chap like that. The Valentine generation. I wonder what May'd say. Not that I'll ever know. There are some things a man keeps to himself. "Was she pretty?" I can just hear her asking. "Must have been, for you to stand there talking to her and get behind with your collections and finish up with risking the sack, and no provision for our old age." No, the only way to get an idea would be to imagine May at that girl's age. She was a real woman. Not much Royal Doulton there.

I wonder.

A Message from the Pig-Man

He was never called Ekky now, because he was getting to be a real boy, nearly six, with grey flannel trousers that had a separate belt and weren't kept up by elastic, and his name was Eric. But this was just one of those changes brought about naturally, by time, not a disturbing alteration; he understood that. His mother hadn't meant that kind of change when she had promised, "Nothing will be changed." It was all going to go on as before, except that Dad wouldn't be there, and Donald would be there instead. He knew Donald, of course, and felt all right about his being in the house, though it seemed, when he lay in bed and thought about it, mad and pointless that Donald's coming should mean that Dad had to go. Why should it mean that? The house was quite big. He hadn't any brothers and sisters, and if he *had* had any he wouldn't have minded sharing his bedroom, even with a baby that wanted a lot of looking after, so long as it left the spare room free for Dad to sleep in. If he did that, they wouldn't have a spare room, it was true, but then the spare room was nearly always empty; the last time anybody had used the spare room was *years* ago, when he had been much smaller – last winter, in fact. And, even then, the visitor, the lady with the funny teeth who laughed as she breathed in, instead of as she breathed out like everyone else, had only stayed two or three nights. *Why* did grown-ups do everything in such a mad, silly way? They often told him not to be silly, but they were silly themselves in a useless way, not laughing or singing or anything, just being silly and sad.

It was so hard to read the signs; that was another thing. When they did give you something to go on, it was impossible to know how to take it. Dad had bought him a train, just a few weeks ago, and taught him how to fit the lines together. That ought to have meant that he would stay; what sensible person would buy a train, and fit it all up ready to run, even as a present for another person – *and then leave?* Donald had been quite good about the train, Eric had to admit that; he had bought a bridge for it and a lot of rolling-stock. At first he had got the wrong kind of rolling-stock, with wheels too close together to fit on to the rails; but instead of playing the usual grown-ups' trick of pulling a face and then not doing anything about it, he had gone back to the shop, straight away that same afternoon, and got the right kind. Perhaps that meant *he* was going to leave. But that didn't seem likely. Not the way Mum held on to him all the time, even holding him round the middle as if he needed keeping in one piece.

All the same, he was not Ekky now, he was Eric, and he was sensible and grown-up. Probably it was his own fault that everything seemed strange. He was not living up to his grey flannel trousers – perhaps that was it; being afraid of too many things, not asking questions that would probably turn out to have quite simple answers.

The Pig-man, for instance. He had let the Pig-man worry him far too much. None of the grown-ups acted as if the Pig-man was anything to be afraid of. He probably just *looked* funny, that was all. If, instead of avoiding him so carefully, he went outside one evening and looked at him, took a good long, unafraid look, leaving the back door open behind him so that he could dart in to safety and warmth of the house...no! It was better, after all, not to see the Pig-man; not till he was bigger, anyway; nearly six was quite big but it wasn't really *very* big...

And yet it was one of those puzzling things. No one ever told him to be careful not to let the Pig-man get hold of him, or warned him in any way; so the Pig-man *must* be harmless, because when it came to anything that *could* hurt you, like the traffic on the main road, people were always ramming it in to you that you must look both ways, and all that stuff. And yet when it came to the Pig-man, no one ever mentioned him; he seemed beneath the notice of grown-ups. His mother would say, now and then, "Let me see, it's today the Pig-man comes, isn't it?" or, "Oh dear, the Pig-man will be coming round soon, and I haven't put anything out." If she talked like this, Eric's spine would tingle and go cold; he would keep very still and wait, because quite often her next words would be, "Eric, just take these peelings," or whatever it was, "out to the bucket, dear, will you?" The bucket was about fifty yards away from the back door; it was shared by the people in the two next-door houses. None of *them* was afraid of the Pig-man, either. What was their attitude, he wondered? Were they sorry for him, having to eat damp old stuff out of a bucket – tea-leaves and eggshells and that sort of thing? Perhaps he cooked it when he got home, and made it a bit nicer. Certainly it didn't look too nice when you lifted the lid of the bucket and saw it all lying there. It sometimes smelt, too. Was the Pig-man very poor? Was he sorry for himself, or did he feel all right about being like that? *Like what?* What did the Pig-man look like? He would have little eyes, and a snout with a flat end; but would he have trotters, or hands and feet like a person's?

Lying on his back, Eric worked soberly at the problem. The Pig-man's bucket had a handle; so he must carry it in the ordinary way, in his hand – unless, of course, he walked on all fours and carried it in his mouth. But that wasn't very likely, because if he walked on all fours, what difference would there be between him and an ordinary pig? To be called the Pig-man, rather than the Man-pig, surely implied that he was upright, and dressed. Could he talk? Probably, in a kind of grunting way, or else how could he tell the people what kind of food he wanted them to put in his bucket? *Why hadn't he asked Dad about the Pig-man?* That had been his mistake; Dad would have told him exactly all about it. But he had gone. Eric fell asleep, and in his sleep he saw Dad and the Pig-man going in a train together; he called, but they did not hear and the train carried them away. "Dad!" he shouted desperately after it. "Don't bring the Pig-man when you come back! Don't bring the Pig-man!" Then his mother was in the room, kissing him and smelling nice; she felt soft, and the softness ducked him into sleep, this time without dreams; but the next day his questions returned.

Still, there was school in the morning, and going down to the swings in the afternoon, and altogether a lot of different things to crowd out the figure of the Pig-man and the questions connected with it. And he was never furthur from worrying about it all than that moment, a few evenings later, when it suddenly came to a crisis.

Eric had been allowed, "just for once", to bring his train into the dining-room after tea, because there was a fire there that made it nicer than the room where he usually played. It was warm and bright, and the carpet in front of the fireplace was smooth and firm, exactly right for laying out the rails on. Donald had come home and was sitting – in Dad's chair, but never mind – reading the paper and smoking. Mum was in the kitchen, clattering gently about, and both doors were open so that she and Donald could call out remarks to each other. Only a short passage lay between. It was just the part of the day Eric liked best, and bedtime was comfortably far off. He fitted the sections of rail together, glancing in anticipation at the engine as it stood proudly waiting to haul the carriages round and round, tremendously fast.

Then his mother called, "Eric! Do be a sweet, good boy, and take this stuff out for the Pig-man. My hands are covered with cake mixture. I'll let you scrape out the basin when you come in."

For a moment he kept quite still, hoping he hadn't really heard her say it, that it was just a voice inside his head. But Donald looked over at him and said, "Go along, old man. You don't mind, do you?"

Eric said, "But to-night's when the Pig-man *comes*."

Surely, *surely* they weren't asking him to go out, in the deep twilight, just at the time when there was the greatest danger of actually *meeting* the Pig-man?

"All the better," said Donald, turning back to his paper.

Why was it better? Did they *want* him to meet the Pig-man?

Slowly, wondering why his feet and legs didn't refuse to move, Eric went through into the kitchen. "There it is," his mother said, pointing to a brown-paper carrier full of potato-peelings and scraps.

He took it up and opened the back door. If he was quick, and darted along to the bucket *at once*, he would be able to lift the lid, throw the stuff in quickly, and be back in the house in about the time it took to count ten.

One – two – three – four – five – six. He stopped. The bucket wasn't there.

It had gone. Eric peered round, but the light, though faint, was not as faint as *that*. He could see that the bucket had gone. *The Pig-man had already been.*

Seven – eight – nine – ten, his steps were joyous and light. Back in the house, where it was warm and bright and his train was waiting.

"The Pig-man's gone, Mum. The bucket's not there."

She frowned, hands deep in the pudding-basin. "Oh, yes, I do believe I heard him. But it was only a moment ago. Yes, it was just before I called you, darling. It must have been that that made me think of it."

"Yes?" he said politely, putting down the carrier.

"So if you nip along, dear, you can easily catch him up. And I *do* want that stuff out of the way."

"Catch him up?" he asked, standing still in the doorway.

"Yes, dear, *catch him up*," she answered rather sharply (the Efficient Young Mother knows when to be Firm). "He can't possibly be more than a very short way down the road."

Before she had finished Eric was outside the door and running. This was a technique he knew. It was the same as getting into icy cold water. If it was the end, if the Pig-man seized him by the hand and dragged him off to his hut, well, so much the worse. Swinging the paper carrier in his hand, he ran fast through the dusk.

The back view of the Pig-man was much as he had expected it to be. A slow, rather lurching gait, hunched shoulders, an old hat crushed down on his head (to hide his ears?) and the pail in his hand. Plod, plod, as if he were tired. Perhaps this was just a ruse, though, probably he could pounce quickly enough when his wicked little eyes saw a nice tasty little boy or something...did the Pig-man eat birds? Or cats?

Eric stopped. He opened his mouth to call to the Pig-man, but the first time he tried, nothing came out except a small rasping squeak. His heart was banging like fireworks going off. He could hardly hear anything.

"Mr Pig-man!" he called, and this time the words came out clear and rather high.

The jogging old figure stopped, turned, and looked at him. Eric could not see properly from where he stood. But he *had* to see. Everything, even his fear, sank and drowned in the raging tide of his curiosity. He moved forward. With each step he saw more clearly. The Pig-man was just an ordinary old man.

"Hello, sonny. Got some stuff there for the old grunters?"

Eric nodded, mutely, and held out his offering. What old grunters? What did he mean?

The Pig-man put down his bucket. He had ordinary hands, ordinary arms. He took the lid off. Eric held out the paper carrier, and the Pig-man's hand actually touched his own for a second. A flood of gratitude rose up inside him. The Pig-man tipped the scraps into the bucket and handed the carrier back.

"Thanks, sonny," he said.

"Who's it for?" Eric asked, with another rush of articulateness. His voice seemed to have a life of its own.

The Pig-man straightened up, puzzled. Then he laughed, in a gurgling sort of way, but not like a pig at all.

"Arh Aarh Harh Harh," the Pig-man went. "Not for me, if that's whatcher mean, arh harh."

He put the lid back on the bucket. "It's for the old grunters," he said. "The old porkers. Just what they likes. Only not fruit skins. I leaves a note, sometimes, about what not to put in. Never fruit skins. It gives 'em the belly-ache.''

He was called the Pig-man because he had some pigs that he looked after.

"Thank you," said Eric. "Good-night." He ran back towards the house, hearing the Pig-man, the ordinary old man, the ordinary usual normal old man, say in his just ordinary old man's voice, "Good-night, sonny."

So that was how you did it. You just went straight ahead, not worrying about this or that. Like getting into cold water. You just *did* it.

He slowed down as he got to the gate. For instance, if there was a question that you wanted to know the answer to, and you had always just felt you couldn't ask, the thing to do was to ask it. Just straight out, like going up to the Pig-man. Difficult things, troubles, questions, you just treated them like the Pig-man.

So that was it!

The warm light shone through the crack of the door. He opened it and went in. His mother was standing at the table, her hands still working the cake mixture about. She would let him scrape out the basin, and the spoon – he would ask for the spoon, too. But not straight away. There was a more important thing first.

He put the paper carrier down and went up to her. "Mum," he said. "Why can't Dad be with us even if Donald *is* here? I mean, why can't he live with us as well as Donald?"

His mother turned and went to the sink. She put the tap on and held her hands under it.

"Darling," she called.

"Yes?" came Donald's voice.

"D'you know what he's just said?"

"What?"

"He's just asked. . ." She turned the tap off and dried her hands, not looking at Eric. "He wants to know why we can't have Jack to live with us."

There was a silence, then Donald said, quietly, so that his voice only just reached Eric's ears, "That's a hard one."

"You can scrape out the basin," his mother said to Eric. She lifted him up and kissed him. Then she rubbed her cheek along his, leaving a wet smear. "Poor little Ekky," she said in a funny voice.

She put him down and he began to scrape out the pudding-basin, certain at least of one thing, that grown-ups were mad and silly and he hated them all, all, *all*.

Down Our Way

"God made us all different. Don't talk back to your mother," said Mr Robinson.

"It's not the blacks I mind. They don't know any better," said Mrs Robinson. "But a man like that, knocking on people's doors and making trouble. There ought to be a law against it."

"I expect there is, come to think of it," said Mr Robinson. "Appearing in disguise on the public highway."

"Not now," said Arthur Robinson, blowing on his tea. "In olden days, yes. But it wouldn't work today. What with all these wigs and that, and not being able to tell whether it's a girl or a boy till you come right up to 'em – " he expelled a harsh blast of air that sent his tea climbing dangerously high up its white glazed wall. "You'd have to put half the country in prison."

"Good job too," said Mrs Robinson. She cut her piece of fruit-cake into sections, vigorously. "They want teaching a good lesson, some of 'em. Dirty little madams."

"The black fellers have got to live, mum," said Doris Robinson with her usual stolid defiance.

"Nobody's stopping them," said Mr Robinson. "They're welcome to live as long as they stay where the good Lord put 'em. But they shouldn't come pouring into a white man's country. That's what I say and I've got the Bible to prove it."

"Some people don't reckon the Bible proves anything," said Doris. "After you, Arthur. I like jam, too."

"They ought to be ashamed, then," said Mrs Robinson. "Dirty colour-blind little madams. They don't care who they're with, so long as it's a man."

"Well, they've got a point," said Doris, attacking the jam.

"Make allowances, mum," said Arthur. "I expect that's what it feels like when you're twenty-six and haven't got a husband yet."

"Why don't you go and give all your blood to the Red Cross?" queried his sister indifferently.

"I bet you'd go out with a darkie fast enough," said Arthur, disappointed at Doris's calm.

"I would if I liked him.'

"You want to read your Bible, my girl," said Mr Robinson, getting up from his chair with slow dignity and going to look for his pipe. "The sons of Ram shall bruise thy heel, and thou shalt bruise his head. Remember that."

"Rough play in the Second Division," said Arthur.

"The blacks can't help it," said Mrs Robinson with a look of determined fair-mindedness. "It's a man like that I'd put in prison. Blacking his face and knocking on people's doors."

"They'll do anything to get a story," said Arthur. "I saw a play about it on the telly. They have to make something happen, else there's nothing to put in the paper."

"They want to mind their own business," said Mr Robinson through a cloud of pipe-smoke. "They'd have plenty to put in the paper if they'd read their Bible."

"Well, it's this neighbourhood," said Doris. "That's what everybody was saying at work today. He's working his way round East London and we can expect him here any time."

"He won't have any trouble with the birds if he comes round this way," said Arthur. "Soon as they see a darkie they start running. Towards him."

"Jealousy, that's your trouble," said Doris. "No wonder you can't keep a girl-friend, with them pimples."

"If they weren't a lot of ignorant little madams," said Mrs Robinson, "they'd sooner have a nice clean English boy than a blackie, even with a few pimples."

"Let's shut up about pimples, shall we?" said Arthur. "I'm having my tea."

"You know what it'll say in the paper next morning, when he knocks on the door and you turn him away," said Doris. "Mr and Mrs Fred Robinson, who've been advertising in their front window with a room to let for the last six months, turned away the very first person that asked about it because he was coloured."

"Who cares what it says in the paper?" Mr Robinson demanded. "An Englishman's home is his castle."

"Does it say that in the Bible?" asked Doris innocently.

"You watch your tongue, Doris," said Mrs Robinson. "That's all I say to you, watch your tongue."

There was a knock at the street door.

"If that's him," said Mr Robinson, "tell him to go home and wash the black off his face."

"And not come making trouble, just to get a story," Arthur

added righteously.

Doris was moving her chair back from the table when she saw that her mother had risen and was going into the passage.

"Be careful what you do, mum," she called.

"I know what I'm about," said Mrs Robinson shortly.

All three listened intently as the door opened and Mrs Robinson's voice came to them down the hallway. But they could make out nothing except an occasional broken phrase, "Don't think so," "I'll tell him," "shouldn't expect." The other voice was a man's, but they caught nothing it said.

After a few minutes Mrs Robinson closed the front door and came back to them.

"Was that him?" Arthur asked.

"No. Mr Prothero," she replied.

"Mr who?"

"The young man from the church. The curate. Mr Venables had sent him round."

"And why didn't Mr Venables come his high and mighty self?" demanded Mr Robinson from beside the fire. "After eight years as sidesman, I'm not worth his while to drop in on his way past?"

"That's what he wanted to talk about," said Mrs Robinson. "Said Mr Venables was sorry to hear you was giving up."

"You told him why, didn't you?"

"Yes. He wanted to come in and talk to you, but I said I couldn't have you bothered. Said the doctor told you to keep out of draughts with your legs. And I asked him straight out, could he deny that the church was draughty?"

"Specially round the sides, where I had to walk," said Mr Robinson. "Eight years I took my legs down the draughtiest part of that church. Enough's enough, I say."

"I never can understand that," said Arthur reflectively. "The church business. The same service going on in hundreds of churches at the same time. Wasting manpower like that, how stupid can you get? They should have one central service and televise it."

"Tune in to channel fourteen and go on your knees on the hearthrug," said Doris satirically.

"Well, there's more sense to that than what they do," said Arthur. "If Dad'd knelt on the hearthrug for thirty years instead of in cold draughty churches, his legs'd be as good as mine now."

"Yours'll never come to any harm through bending your

knees, that I will say," Mr Robinson remarked.

"Never mind all that," said Mrs Robinson, who had been thinking. "This man. If he comes, I've decided what to do."

"You'd better take the notice down, till the whole thing's over," said Mr Robinson.

"No. That'd be running away. I've got a better idea. Welcome him."

"*Welcome* –" Arthur was beginning astonishment.

"Pretend to take him for a real darkie. After all, it's only by chance that we know about it. Nothing's been in the paper yet. I'll pretend not to suspect anything, be as nice as pie. That'll take the wind right out of his sails, make him drop the whole silly idea."

"Ask him for a week's rent in advance. He'll have plenty of expense money," said Mr Robinson.

Doris began to clear away the dishes. "I think it's childish, if you ask me," she said into the air.

"Childish?" said her mother. "Who started it? What's more childish than blacking your face and knocking on people's doors?"

There was another knock, and she hurried down the passage; it was the next-door neighbour, wanting to borrow a cookery book. A few minutes later she ran to the door again, and made short work of a salesman proffering details of an encyclopaedia. The atmosphere of expectancy began to leak away; Mr Robinson, dozing over the evening paper, had almost dismissed the matter from his mind.

But after half a hour the summons again. Mrs Robinson grumbled her way to the front door without haste, but this time she was longer in coming back, and the family were roused into sudden attentiveness by the bright, welcoming tones of her voice, which now reached them clearly.

"This way, will you please? I'd like you to meet Mr Robinson and our son and daughter...we're all at home...This is the front room, we've just cleared away our tea...This way." She entered looking, over her shoulder at someone who was following her, and making little mincing movements of her head and body that made her look like a clumsily operated puppet.

Mr Robinson, Arthur and Doris all turned their eyes expectantly towards the doorway. At once, they were rewarded with a sight that froze them rigid with sheer surprise and, in the case of Arthur, with fury.

The newcomer was a stocky, broad-faced West Indian wearing

a startlingly white raincoat and carrying a shiny plastic cap in his hand. The raincoat, as perhaps it was meant to do, concealed the clothes he was wearing under it, except for the bottom of his trousers, which appeared to be fairly voluminous at calf-level and caught in sharply at the ankles. His shoes were cracked, but clean and polished. As he came through the door, he looked cautiously from face to face and said, "Good evening to all."

"It's lucky the family are all at home," said Mrs Robinson brightly. "Then we can all get acquainted at once. This is Arthur, this is Doris, and this our Dad, Mr Robinson. They're all out at work all day and the young ones seem to be out most of the nights as well, but you know what young people are these days. Of course it's up to you whether you go out in the evenings or stay in your room – you're quite free to suit yourself entirely."

"Thank you, missis," said the man. His brown face split in a gleaming smile. "Can I see the room now?"

"I'll take you up," said Mrs Robinson. "It's a nice quiet room with a bay window on the street. This is a very quiet street, I expect you've noticed. Never a bit of noise from traffic or the neighbours. Of course it's a very quiet neighbourhood. I *have* been told as I ought to charge ten shillings a week extra for the quiet, as an amenity, sort of thing, but I don't. What I say is, if we have the luck to live in a nice quiet street, we'll share our good fortune with other people. Excuse me, I'll lead the way."

She went out and up the stairs, followed by the stranger. Hardly had the man's broad back vanished through the doorway, when Arthur let out a prolonged whistle of astonishment.

"Phe-e-e-e-ew!" He mopped his brow. "She really thinks it's him."

"She can't do," said his sister.

"She *must* do. That's why she's sweet-talking him. Wants him to go away and write in the paper what a nice welcome he found at 46, Crescent Street. She's mad! She's mad! What'll she do when she finds out?"

"Well," said Mr Robinson, retiring behind the paper, "she'll have to do something. I want no part of this. She got him in and she'll get him out."

Footsteps bumped down the stairs.

"I'm glad to say," Mrs Robinson beamed, "that Mr – er –"

"Major. Samuel Henry Major."

"That Mr Major likes the room and he's going to take it. When would you like to come in, Mr Major?"

"Tomorrow, please, missis. I'll bring my cases over in the afternoon. I've got one more night to go in the place I'm staying now. I've paid up to the Wednesday and I don't want to give him a golden handshake." Again the grin flashed out.

Mrs Robinson, standing behind Mr Major, threw a triumphant glance at her family. Her dignified face did not lend itself to anything as playful as winking; nevertheless, it conveyed the suggestion of a wink. "Look at me leading him up the garden path!" her expression said.

Two ferocious scowls (male) and one look of pure pity (female) flashed back at her. The whole exchange took approximately one second.

"I've told Mr Major our terms," Mrs Robinson went on. "Three pounds a week or three pounds fifteen with light house-keeping."

Mr Robinson snatched the pipe out of his mouth and said quickly, "But when we discussed it you said – "

"Never mind," Mrs Robinson interrupted him with equal haste. "I like to keep our charges reasonable. What I say is, we've had good luck – let's share it with others." And once again she gave that quick glance of complicity.

Mr Robinson, defeated, took up the paper again. This left Arthur as the only defender of the citadel. He stared insolently at Mr Major. "Are you taking the room just for yourself? Or bringing anybody else in?"

"My family are back home," said Mr Major. "In Trinidad," he explained. "Here is their photograph. Three boys and a girl. My wife will bring them when I save the money, like." He took a photograph from his wallet and held it out to Arthur, who frowned and kept his arms by his sides. After a moment Doris took the photograph from Mr Major's hand and looked at it.

"What a nice family," she said, "I expect they miss you."

"Photographs!" said Mrs Robinson's expression. "The lengths these newspapers will go to!"

"*I* miss *them* every day," said Mr Major simply. "That's why I'm glad to get a room so reasonable. I'm saving every shilling I get. The fare is a lot of money. But," he smiled, "I'll make it."

"This the first place you've tried?" Arthur had not taken his hard stare from Mr Major's face.

"No. I tried several before," said Mr Major briefly.

"Wouldn't have you, I suppose?" Arthur pursued.

"They were full up," said Mr Major. His face was without

expression.

A silence filled the room. Mrs Robinson seemed to be debating inwardly whether to throw down the gauntlet and tell the man she knew he was a reporter and not a West Indian at all. Perhaps to avert the hideous farce this would involve, Doris asked nervously, "Do you find it lonely over here?"

"Why, you got any suggestions?" said Arthur in a savage undertone.

"I go to the Social Club a lot," said Mr Major, ignoring Arthur's question or not hearing it. "I have lots of friends down there. Corner of Hubbard Street and Acacia Street. They get a very nice type. No need to spend money. I just drink a cup of tea and I stay and chat with my friends. I tell them, when my family comes over I'll give up tea for a while and celebrate with them."

There was another silence, and Mr Major finally said, "I'll be off down there now. Thank you very much, missis. I'll bring my cases along tomorrow night."

"Where d'you work?" Mr Robinson suddenly asked, as if to pin down a vital piece of information before it was too late.

"On the electric," said Mr Major. Evidently feeling this reply to be sufficiently meaningful, he smiled again, said "Good night to all," and retreated along the hall-way, his shoulder brushing the wall as he went past the umbrella-stand.

The door closed behind him, and the Robinsons were left in an unnatural silence and stillness: the entire family seemed to have shrunk to four pairs of eyes, three accusing and one defensive.

"All right, go on, mother," said Mr Robinson at last. "Tell us how you're going to get out of this one."

"What is there to get out of?" Mrs Robinson asked stonily, but with a curious deadness in her voice which indicated that she was playing for time.

"You know good and well what there is to get out of!" Arthur's voice came out high-pitched and unsteady. "You've gone and let the room to a real nigger. You thought you'd be clever and take a rise out the man, and you've ended up with a nigger in the house along with your own family."

Doris got up abruptly. "I'm off out," she said. "I'll leave you clever ones to sort it out among yourselves. P'raps Dad can find the answer in the Bible."

"You leave the Bible out of this, my girl," said Mr Robinson severely. "There's no call to be blasphemous – bringing the Bible in where it's no call to be."

"How are you so sure that isn't the man with his face blacked?" Mrs Robinson persisted feebly.

"Oh, get your glasses changed, Mum," Arthur snapped. His forehead was red with the enormous anger inside him. "If you can look at a face like his and still think the colour'd *wash off*, you must be more stupid than you look."

"Don't talk to me like that," his mother rallied, glad to have some familiar ground to stand on. "Stupid, is it? You'd all be in a right mess without me, even if I am stupid. Sometimes I think I'll walk out and see how you all get on, you – "

"Don't let's get on the argy-bargy," said Mr Robinson, raising his hand like a traffic policeman. "Arthur, don't talk like that to your mother. And you, mother don't take any notice of him. He's overstrained. What we want to know is, how are we going to get out of this mess?"

"That's right," said Arthur fiercely. "Mess is right. The first darkie to come knocking at the door and we take him straight in. Beat that for a mess."

Doris, who had been upstairs to change her dress, came down and poked her head in at the door of the living-room.

"Well?" she said brightly. "Figured your way out of it yet?"

"Don't worry," said Mrs Robinson with dignity, "I'll take another look at him when he comes back, and if it's true that I've made a mistake – I say *if* it's true – I'll soon get rid of him."

"How?" Doris asked. Her voice lost its lightness and she drew her brows together. "What d'you mean?"

"You don't think I'm really going to have a darkie in my house?" asked Mrs Robinson simply.

Doris looked for a long moment at her mother's impassive face. Then, silent, she turned and went down the hallway. The front door banged.

"What's the scheme, then, Mum?" asked Arthur. He felt in his jacket pocket for cigarettes, and looked across at her hopefully.

"When he comes back," said Mrs Robinson, "I shall just tell him there's been a mistake and he can't have the room after all."

"A mistake?" Arthur was disappointed. "What kind of a mistake would that be, then? How can it be all right for him to have the room one evening, and not all right the next? You'll have to do better than that."

"Yes, mother," Mr Robinson umpired from his armchair, "you'll have to give him a reason."

"Reason?" said Mrs Robinson massively, "*reason?* whose house is it?"

"You've offered a room to let," said Mr Robinson, "a man's taken it, and even if he is a blackie you can't just tell him you've changed your mind.

"Think what the papers'd print about *that*," said Arthur. "He'd go straight and sell 'em the story for fifty quid. They know where the money is."

"All right," said Mrs Robinson placidly. "P'raps we'll have to have him in the place for a day or two. But it won't be long. He'll soon put a foot wrong and as soon as he does I'll have him out."

"Put a foot wrong?" Arthur queried. "Like how?"

"Like anything at all," said Mrs Robinson. "The lodger never lived who didn't leave the bathroom dirty, or smoke in bed or make a noise taking his boots off at night, or have undesirables in his room. If you take a lodger, you have to make all sorts of allowances or else you'd be asking him to move out within three days. Well, this one'll be on his way quicker than that." She gave a short, scornful laugh. "I haven't lived fifty years to end up not being mistress in my own house."

Arthur, contented, lit his cigarette and began to fiddle with the television set. Mr Robinson, holding the evening paper on his knee, looked over at his wife's face. For the first time in twenty years, he looked at Mrs Robinson and really saw her. Then, slowly, his eyes dropped and he went on reading the paper.

Goodnight, Old Daisy

"I've told you before, you're welcome to stop at home father," said Mrs Foster. Her voice was righteous but with an undertone of exasperation. "If you want to spend your days hanging about in that draughty place, you've only got yourself to blame."

"Blame for what?" Mr Greeley asked mildly. He was moving slowly towards the front door, buttoning up his macintosh: his cap and muffler were already on.

"If you catch your death, of course." said Mrs Foster. "You've got a warm comfortable home here, and goodness knows it costs me and Cyril enough trouble and money to keep it up. You could sit by the fire and read the paper, and no one to disturb you, as long as the children are at school, and they stay to dinner now." She swept her duster in a wide arc across the already dustfree sideboard. "And you have to go out every blessed day, down to that draughty place. If you lived in the workhouse I could understand it."

Mr Greeley paused, deeply considering her words.

"It was my life Nora," he said at last. "I don't go down there to annoy you. But I don't want to sit by the fire all the time. I like to go down and see the old girl. It was my life, remember."

"Well, I won't hinder you if that's your idea of enjoying yourself," said Mrs Foster. "I've told you you're welcome to stop at home. At least it's warm here, and with the cost of heating what it is that's something, I should think. Even if you don't appreciate it."

Mr Greeley turned his weak old eyes on his daughter and faced her with a faded dignity that recalled the fine man he had once been, though not to Mrs Foster, who did not remember a time when she had not considered him old and worn-out.

"We've had this before Nora," he said. "If I like to go down and look at the old girl, well, that's not to say I don't regard the kindness you show me in giving me a home, you and Cyril."

"When you catch your death, you'll come to me to be nursed," she said, polishing. "They don't keep that place warm enough."

"I've never coddled myself," said Mr Greeley. "If I should fall ill, send me to hospital. You won't ever have to nurse me."

Straightening his shoulders, he marched defiantly to the door and out. The tension produced by his daughter's nagging had caused his heart to beat fast, sending his thin blood coursing through its channels, but this did little enough to warm him against the icy wind that blew round the unsheltered bus stop. He drew his macintosh tightly round him; much worn and threadbare, it was better than nothing, and he could not afford to buy himself a new coat and would not ask his daughter for the money.

While Mr Greeley waited, several other people gathered at the bus stop, and one of them, a woman in her thirties, greeted him.

"Going to town, Mr Greeley?"

"Just to the Collection," he replied. "I generally go down and have a look at the old girl."

Furred and scarfed against the wind, she looked at him uncomprehendingly. Nora's old dad. She'd seen him in the background when she and Don went round for an evening. Nice of Cyril to put up with him really, and him pretty near ga-ga. The Collection? What did he mean?

"That's right," she said vaguely, her gaze travelling past the old man in search of something interesting enough to hold her attention.

The bus coming into view, spared her any further social effort. When it halted, the knot of waiters, elevated now to the dignity of passengers, climbed thankfully into its warm interior.

"The Collection return," said Mr Greeley to the conductor.

The railway museum was officially known as the Phipps Historical Railway Collection, in honour of some long-dead director who gave funds to start it, and Mr Greeley considered it beneath the Collection's dignity to be known as anything else. Some of the bus conductors knew what he meant, others did not; but by persevering he hoped, in time, to instruct them all.

This morning the conductor, a youth of about twenty, seemed not; but by persevering he hoped, in time, to instruct them all. sengers and then returned with, "Where to dad?"

"The Phipps Memorial Collection. Ducker Street," said Mr Greeley, with careful distinctness.

"Oh, Ducker Street," said the lad carelessly. "5p."

"*Return*," said Mr Greeley doggedly.

"Oh, return. 9p."

Mr Greeley already had the coins in his hand; he paid up and sank back into his own thoughts. Ducker Street! The conductor had it seemed, heard of the street and not the Collection. Yet the street was a short one, a mere link between two main streets at the centre of the town, and there was hardly anything else there except the Collection. But it was the street you ask for. A triviality, yet a straw that showed how the wind blew. Forget-fulness, forgetfulness everywhere: the great days, the great doings, blown away on the gritty wind.

The bus halted at Ducker Street, and Mr Greeley got out and stood for a moment on the pavement. The Collection was beside the station, whose main entrance was two streets away. From the station Mr Greeley could hear the clash of wagons being shunted. Drawn by the sound, he hesitated. But what was the use? There was no hiss or chuff to be heard, not a plume of white to be seen; the station had been modernised and there were no steam locomotives working now.

And diesels...Mr Greeley had no objections to diesels in their own way, but there was no interest in watching them. Who wanted to watch a lot of steel boxes moving about?

He went up the steps of the Collection and hurried in. The large, whitewashed building was not very warm, but it seemed so after the chill of the street, and it was possible to take off one's overcoat without discomfort. Mr Greeley did so, but kept on his cap and muffler. Hanging up his macintosh, he turned to greet the attendant who usually sat on a chair inside the door, a taciturn, grizzled man whom he had grown to like. But instead of the familiar attendant, a new and youthful face looked at him from under a peaked cap.

"Where's Ernie?" Mr Greeley asked.

"He's off sick," the stripling replied. "I'm doing his job till he gets back." He made no further explanation of himself: what his normal job was, where his peaked cap came from (Ernie never wore one), and how he could be spared to take over from Ernie. Was he a trainee? Was Ernie's job being kept warm for him? He was a non-explainer, a budding authoritarian. Mistrusting him, Mr Greeley moved away.

Never mind! Attendant or no attendant, here she was, and here she would always be. The Phipps Collection was not very large; a few old wagons, a glass case or two containing old railwaymen's uniforms and tools, a couple of narrow-gauge engines standing one behind the other on a stretch of antique track, and a number of scale models of historic engines, some of which, if you fed them a penny, whirred sadly into action for a little while. But all these were accompaniments, grouped on the margin.

The pride of the Collection, the one big, important item that made it worth calling a Collection at all, stood firmly in the middle. Her brass gleamed, her paint shone, her majestic size drew the eye of everyone who entered. She was a gigantic green-and-gold engine of the 4–6–o type, complete with her eight wheeled tender. Over her huge driving wheels, brass letters proclaimed her official name, which was that of a castle. But Mr Greeley, in the years when he and this giantess had lived their lives together, had always called her Daisy. He could not have said why; Daisy just seemed to suit her. In his long dialogues with her, as she swayed and hissed and thundered, and the riveted metal plates shivered under his feet, Mr Greeley had simply found himself calling her Daisy, and that was that.

He drew his hand along the edge of her long platform.

"Hello Daisy," he said softly. "Another morning, old girl." Daisy stood impassive: she had no means of replying. Yet Mr Greeley did not feel that it was artificial, or even eccentric, to speak to her. Their relationship had been a living one: he had fed strength into her veins, causing her to leap and sway, heaving hundreds of tons of solid matter into urgent, clattering motion. And at the end of the run his hand had shut off her steam, calmed her, cradled her into her metallic sleep. And now she was sleeping for ever. But he was too sensible a man to fight against his own subjective feelings and his feelings told him that he was her driver, and would always be her driver, and to her he could never be as other men were.

Stiffly, Mr Greeley clambered up Daisy's steps and into that cab in which he had spent thousands of hours. Taking out a soft duster, he carefully polished the brass fittings that made up Daisy's intelligence, her nerve centre, the seat of her personality. Then he straightened up and took a long, calm look out of the window, first on the platform side, then on the off side.

All was clear. Except for a small, meaningless commotion on the floor of the Collection. A little figure with jerky movements, looking like an insect beside the monumental locomotive, was scurrying towards them. It was the new attendant.

"No standing on the exhibits, please," he barked, hurrying. Drawing near, his face came to the level of Mr Greeley's boots. "I must have you down, please."

"Down?" said Mr Greeley incredulously. Could he believe what his ears told him? Down? Him?

"There's a notice up," said the youth firmly. "We can't allow the public to climb up on the exhibits."

"I'm not the public, lad," said Mr Greeley. "I was this engine's regular driver in the last thirty years of her life." He spoke forgivingly: after all it was the boy's first day on the job.

"Please come down," the young attendant repeated. His face was pale and stern: he might have been defending the grey head of a parent against outrage. The Collection might have been a cathedral, in danger from a barbaric horde. "Look, the regulations —"

"Fetch the Superintendent;" Mr Greeley commanded loudly. "Go on, fetch him! I won't deal with you!"

At this moment the Superintendent, roused by the sound of their voices, appeared at the door of his office. Having many other duties, he spent only two days a week at the Collection: but this was one of his days and Mr Greeley knew that it was.

"What's the trouble, Perkins?" he asked, taking off his glasses with a weary gesture that was characteristic of him. He was a tall distinguished-looking man, prematurely white-haired, and with that air of polite absence of mind that grows on museum officials. He could be softly polite to whomsoever he was listening or talking to, while at the same time demonstrably thinking of something else.

"Public climbing on the exhibits, sir," said Perkins stiffly. He stood like a lance-corporal.

"Dear me," said the Superintendent gently. "That's not the public, it's Mr Greeley. He spent so long in the cab of that engine that we make an exception for him. How are you today, Mr Greeley?"

"I'm in good shape, Superintendent," Mr Greeley smiled. "But Daisy's in better."

The Superintendent nodded gravely. His mind was already back in his office, looking at balance sheets. "All the better for seeing you Mr Greeley," he said, and turned to go back.

"My mistake, sir," said Perkins, challenging the Superintendent to make some wrapping-up comment.

"We all make them, Perkins," said the Superintendent vaguely. The reply did not satisfy Perkins, who had expected to be absolved and into the bargain congratulated on his zeal. He glared briefly at Mr Greeley, then turned and walked away after the Superintendent.

"Public," said Mr Greeley to Daisy, bitterly. "I hope we can get Ernie back. He knows what's what." He polished some of Daisy's array of brass tubes. "You don't think I'm the public, eh, old girl?"

Mr Greeley's calm had been badly shaken, but half an hour of tranquil communion with Daisy restored it. Stepping briskly, he went across the street to "The Viaduct", a public house he had frequented for fifty years. There, he enjoyed his usual midday meal: a pint of beer and a sandwich. As he ate, and took slow meditative pulls at his beer, Mr Greeley looked around at the juke-box, the tubular steel furniture, the pornographic advertisements for non-alcoholic drinks. The place had changed beyond recognition. He had known it when it was a classic railwayman's pub. Hard-working shunters and oilers, yes, even humble porters in their shorn-off jackets, had rubbed shoulders at the bar with the drivers of famous trains. Including Mr Greeley himself.

Often and often had he come striding quickly into the pub with a raging thirst, flinging down on the polished bar a handful of small change that was almost too hot to touch. The fierce heat from Daisy's firebox used to make his overalls so hot that they were all but scorched. And how he sweated! And with what lovely, prodigal gulps had he poured down his throat pints, quarts, yes, even gallons on occasion, of the good beer always on tap at the Viaduct!

The beer seemed to have lost its flavour these days. But then, Mr Greeley reflected, he did not come to it straight from Daisy's cab, with his senses drugged by speed and roaring wind, his skin wet and his throat dry. Beer! it was not just beer in those days, it was benediction. Sighing, but inwardly happy because strengthened and warmed by these memories, Mr Greeley drank the last inch of his weak, flat pint and walked to the door, nodding to the licensee.

Back at the Collection, Mr Greeley swung himself, once more, up the steps of Daisy's cab. From up here, the world looked sane and comely. Even if there was no track stretching ahead, even if all you could see was the concrete floor of the Collection, and opposite you the whitewashed brick wall. Well, that was how the world had gone. It had shrunk, and become flat and grey and washed-out. But at least he and Daisy were both still here.

"Nobody'll ever drive you again, old girl," he said to her, bending his head so that his voice lingered intimately about her proud immobile controls. "I was the last, and I saw you out. And I was the only one that knew what you could really do. When you wanted to, that is, old Daisy!"

Silently, in his mind, he rehearsed the beloved statistics. Heating surface, two thousand and fifty square feet. Weight, fifty-eight tons seventeen hundredweight. The figures gleamed in his mind like the words of some immortal lyric. In their hedged-in statements they contained the whole of his working life: fifty years of eye and sinew.

Work is the misfortune of Adam, laid on man by a vengeful God: Mr Greeley in his time had cursed the alarm clock, coughed on dark mornings, ached as he waited at the icy bus-stop: but never once had he climbed up into Daisy's cab without a flicker of life-giving excitement, a quickening nervous tremor at the root of his heart.

A suppressed burst of tittering, not quite so suppressed as to be inaudible to his old ears, caused Mr Greeley to look up from his reverie. Standing by Daisy's front buffers, peering round at his face, as it was framed in the driver's window, stood two children, a girl of perhaps ten and a boy some three years older.

"Now can you hear him?" the girl asked her brother. Mr Greeley guessed that she had overheard him talking to himself and wanted her brother to share this exquisite joke.

Seeing Mr Greeley's eye on him, the boy dropped all furtiveness and came boldly along beside Daisy's driving-wheels, which towered above him with their imperious height of nearly six feet. He looked directly into Mr Greeley's face, as if about to start a conversation.

Mr Greeley, forgiving the girlish insolence of the sister, smiled benignly down. The boy reminded him of so many similar boys, school-capped and macintoshed, over the years. How they had longed for a few words with the driver of a crack locomotive! And even now, even in the shorn glory of the Collection, it seemed that the feeling was still alive.

"Nice engine, isn't she?" he volunteered, to he'p the boy over his shyness. "I was her driver. She was built in 1914. I was built some time before that, so I am older'n she is." He smiled warmly. Then he noticed the boy's eyes. They were like two stones.

"Anything up to two hundred tons, we used to pull," Mr

Greeley proffered. Then, under the stare of those two utterly unforgiving eyes, he stopped and turned away. What was the use? The boy was beyond his gravitational pull. What had drawn him to visit the Collection at all, Mr Greeley could not imagine. What was clear was his complete and final unwillingness to consider Mr Greeley as a living being of the same species as himself. Contempt, backed by a hard curiosity, had been the message of those eyes. Instead of feeling any thrill at finding himself in the presence of a man who had driven a locomotive capable of hauling two hundred tons, shooting steam high into the air, thrusting and drumming with all that wonderful lyric energy, the boy had behaved more like a particularly heartless biologist noting the reactions of some repulsive creature under vivisection.

Mr Greeley sighed. He did not understand the world as it was now. Perhaps he had never understood it very well. Daisy had been his means of understanding the world; she had transplanted all experience into terms of load, gradient, pressure, curves and adhesion. So arranged, he had been able to grasp it and make sense of it. And boys like this one with his hard blue eyes, escaped from their prosperous homes on Christmas holiday or August excursions, had recognised his authority and bowed to it. But now...well, everything passed. Daisy was younger than he was, but their working life had ended at the same time. Only her museum life, that long lonely twilight, would go on longer than his. But let no child look at her as this one had looked at him!

Climbing sadly down, Mr Greeley passed an hour listlessly peering at the other exhibits in the Collection. Shadows began to gather: the misguided young attendant, loftily ignored by Mr Greeley, switched on the lighting.

It was almost time to go back and face his daughter and her family. For some reason Mr Greeley found it even more difficult then usual to accept this necessity. He felt a blind urge to hide himself in some dark corner of the Collection, wait until everyone had gone home, and then come out and spend the night in blissful, unhampered converse with Daisy. But he knew such thoughts were fantastic. At half past five, he fetched his overcoat, put it on and buttoned it. Then, quickly, he mounted Daisy's steps one more time.

"Don't worry, girl," he admonished her. "They'll learn. They'll respect you if they don't respect me. And I'm quite happy, see? I don't matter, you know." He smoothed his hand gently over her brass wheels and levers. "Good night, old Daisy," he said.

Outside, the street was dark. Mr Greeley had to wait a long time for a bus. A light, almost freezing rain was falling. Back at Mrs Foster's house, he had very little appetite for supper.

"You generally like egg and chips, father," said Mrs Foster reproachfully.

"Can I have Grandad's?" asked her watchful son.

"I think I'll turn in," said Mr Greeley.

Lying in his narrow bed, Mr Greeley felt that his bones were weightless, airy. Rising, he slumbered near the ceiling. The wind that stirred the curtain's edge caused him to waver. Then, through air that rocked like water, he was at the bus stop again. A bus was already waiting.

"The Collection," said Mr Greeley firmly holding out a golden sovereign.

"Sorry, you'll have to ask the driver," said the conductor with the faintest hint of condescension. Without wasting words on him, Mr Greeley moved straight up to where a small window gave access to the driver. Poking his head in, Mr Greeley hissed into the driver's ear, "The Collection".

"Where's that?" said the driver, half turning in his seat. He turned no further, because Mr Greeley's powerful hands came through the aperture and gripped his throat.

The driver choked and struggled, but Mr Greeley said, "Follow my directions. Straight on here. Left here. Round this crossing. Right here, right again." His fingers twined lovingly round the driver's windpipe. The driver, well-fleshed and soft to the touch, drove with imploring care. Passengers at intermediate stops were left bewildered and abandoned.

The bus reached Ducker Street, slowed, and stopped. Only then did Mr Greeley unclasp his hands from the driver's plump throat.

"Remember next time, mate," he said grimly. "When someone says the Collection, go there and no messing."

He left the bus with stiff dignity and walked up the steps and into the Collection. It was closed, empty and silent, but a bright moon hung in the sky, and for some reason was able to shine straight down on to the pale concrete floor. Looking up, Mr Greeley saw that the roof of the Collection had gone. The building was open to the warm summer night: for summer had abruptly supplanted winter during the wild and perilous bus ride.

Soft air caressed the engines, the trucks, the lamps and uniforms, the glass cases. Daisy's brasswork gleamed triumphantly in the mellow light. Seen under the moon, she seemed more colossal than in daylight.

Mr Greeley hurried across the floor of the Collection and climbed into Daisy's cab.

"Steam up, by Heaven!" he exclaimed in excitement.

Daisy's firebox glowed hot, her pipes sang, the needles of her pressure gauge crept slowly from left to right.

Then Mr Greeley noticed that his overalls and his shiny black leather cap were hanging in the corner of the cab, on the hook where he had always hung them.

"We're due out!" he said. And all at once it came back to him. "The seven-fifty down!"

His hands, steady and capable, went out to Daisy's heavy brass controls. A few calculated turns on this wheel, a sharp downward pull on that lever. The wheels came into motion. Daisy's whole frame heaved and shook with excitement as her massive connecting-rods began to slide back and forth.

"Where's Ginger?" Mr Greeley asked irritably. He looked round for the fireman he had had on his first runs in 1920. Then he remembered. It wasn't Ginger, it was young Herbert. Or was it Harry Jackson? the last one.

Twisting round, he saw a figure crouched beside the coal, shovel in hand. The stance was Harry Jackson's. That was how Harry had always stood, shovel at the ready, one calculating eye on the firebox door. But the face was Ginger's.

"You've come back, Ginger," said Mr Greeley calmly.

"Yes, gaffer," said Ginger. "I wanted to be by the firebox again. It's cold out there."

Out where? Mr Greeley wondered. But he turned his attention to the controls again.

Daisy was rising easily into the air, floating steadily upwards. The Collection fell away behind them, and Mr Greeley thought he glimpsed the Superintendent standing alone in the space Daisy had occupied, looking up at them wonderingly, fumbling in his upper pocket for his glasses.

Then there was a jolt as Daisy's wheels hit the track. There it was, stretching ahead of them in the glorious moonlight – a mile, three miles, five, ten miles of straight rails.

"The road!" Mr Greeley breathed. He fed Daisy more pressure. And more. And more. The miles whipped by, and Mr Greeley and Ginger shouted for joy in the shuddering cab.

"She's pulling a treat!" Ginger called.

"Clean!" Mr Greeley shouted.

He remembered now. Daisy had been in for servicing. Her boiler had been scraped out. He could never understand why clean water left so much deposit, but it did. Well, they had done a fine job. She had never pulled more smoothly.

"A hundred and seventy," said Mr Greeley to himself, looking at the pressure gauge. "Well why not?" And he increased the pressure till the needle stood at a hundred and eighty.

"Better stop there," said Mr Greeley. He peered ahead through his window. The track stretched away into an inviting landscape of trees and fields. No curves of less than two mile's radius on the whole stretch. He remembered it; his favourite run. But what was different about it? Oh yes – the housing estates had gone. These woods and meadows had been gradually shovelled away, during the years he and Daisy had travelled that road, and hundreds of little brick boxes had sprung up, connected by concrete ribbons and, towered over by glaring arc-lights. Now, all that was gone, the trees waved softly in the moonlight and threw their shadows on to the broad fields.

Mr Greeley blew Daisy's whistle, and he could imagine the sound echoing to lonely farmhouses along with the bark of a fox and the cry of an owl.

But it was no mystery. The time that had bowed him to old age was rolled back, he and Daisy were young again, the trees had not been cut down and the meadows still gleamed under the moon. Rolling up his sleeves, Mr Greeley noticed at once that his arms were more fully fleshed. The stringy old man's muscles had rounded out into the firm, contoured strength he had once taken for granted. And all at once Mr Greeley knew that he would never be old again. He stood straighter, he saw more clearly. Daisy, in all her thundering power and bulk, seemed to submit to him like a bride. And back home he knew Marion waited for him. This evening, at the end of the run back, he would get the bus home and Marion would be waiting. He would take off his working clothes, and wash, and eat, and later that night they would love each other as they used to do.

Daisy rolled easily along at sixty miles an hour, her pressure steady at a hundred and eighty. The track went into a long, full speed curve, and Mr Greeley took the opportunity to look back and see the train they were pulling. Twelve coaches and a guard's van.

"Thirteen," said Mr Greeley and grinned. That was a superstition that had never bothered him.

Daisy's smoke plumed above them, the steel plates shuddered beneath, the dark trees flew by, and the wind roared past their ears. Ginger leaned on his shovel, and he and Mr Greeley grinned at each other with utter contentment. Soon the run would be over; in some unexplained way, in fact, they were already on the return trip, and Marion would be putting the pie in the oven and beginning to watch for the bus that would bring him home. Home? Home.

Standing over Mr Greeley, the young doctor shook his head to Mrs Foster and her husband.

"His resistance is weak," he said, "You can't expect anything else at his age. We can get him into an oxygen tent, and he might rally or he might not." He rubbed his eyes. It was a continual annoyance to him that people seemed to wait for his turn on night duty before deciding to die. Why couldn't they die at weekends?

"We must do everything we can, of course," said Cyril Foster. Inside, he felt a sensation of lightness and relief of which he had the grace to feel slightly ashamed. With the old man gone, that back room could be very useful. The children could have it as a rumpus room. They'd always wanted a rumpus room.

Things happened very quickly after that. Mrs Foster shed a few genuine tears. Their eldest child, Arlene appeared on the landing and was shooed back to bed by Mr Foster. "Poor old dad," Mrs Foster whimpered. "They didn't keep any heating on in that place."

"Course of nature; seventy-five years is a long time." said the doctor.

"Good night old Daisy," said Mr Greeley.

The ambulance arrived. Mr Foster went down and opened the door. The ambulance men joked as they came up the stairs. They got Mr Greeley on to a stretcher and carefully started to go back the way they had come. Arlene appeared again and was whisked back to bed by Mrs Foster. Mr Greeley died. Mr Foster held the front door open as the ambulance men carried the stretcher gently out. The doctor said, "He may rally or he may not."

And the great locomotive, standing silent and imprisoned on the cold grey floor of the Collection, entered another phase of its history.

Points for Discussion

Suggestions for your own writing are marked with an asterisk.

The Life Guard

1 In what ways is the environment of Red Rocks, despite its seaside setting, discouraging to young people? How does it affect the development of Hopper and of Jimmy? But for the tragedy, how might both Hopper's and Jimmy's futures have turned out?

2 P.C. Walker, after Hopper's death, tells Jimmy that "if it does turn out that his heart was weak, that'll let you out of course...no dereliction of duty" (page 21). Do you think that the concept of duty as a life guard had ever *really* been considered by Jimmy? Discuss carefully Jimmy's motives for agreeing to become a life guard, his feelings and reactions during his period as a life guard, and his motives for staging the mock-rescue of Hopper.

3 To what extent was Mr Prendergast's vigorous work with the Development Group motivated by self-interest? Would the community of Red Rocks benefit from his work in any way? To what extent, if any, could he be held responsible for the pattern of events leading to Hopper's death?

4 The episode of Jimmy's real rescue attempt in this story provides a tense and moving climax. It is probably made the more realistic because the reader feels at this stage that he knows the Red Rocks setting and the major characters sufficiently well to be able to identify with the characters and with the setting. Examine the ways in which John Wain has previously in the story built up in his reader's mind a feeling of the physical presence of the sea at Red Rocks and a feeling of the atmosphere of this third-rate resort. You might also examine the ways in which John Wain, by his selection of detail, tends to make his readers adopt his own reactions as their own. Mr Prendergast, for instance, "preferred to give his energy to thinking of ways of increasing

his income" (page 7). And the only amenities actually named at Red Rocks are the High Hat Ballroom and Owen's Fish and Chip Saloon.

5 Fiction often deals with the material of one's instinctive fears of, for instance, heights, open or confined spaces, and water. Discuss the appeal to one's instinctive fear of the sea in "The Life Guard".

6 * Try to project this story from the present final sentence, "Whatever happened, he knew that he would soon be leaving", to the point at which Jimmy does leave, describing local reactions and Jimmy's period of agony.

7 * Describe the ways in which your local environment has conditioned your life and your attitudes to life so far.

Manhood

8 In "The Life Guard", "Swimming was Jimmy's great happiness" (page 4), and it was to achieve a sense of fulfilment for himself that he felt that "he must find someone among this lot, or among one of these lots one of these days, who wanted to be taught to swim. Or, better still, needed to have their life saved" (page 8). But in "Manhood" Rob is certainly not seeking fulfilment for himself, either in cycling, boxing, or rugby. Examine very carefully Mr Willison's explanation to his wife of his reasons for pushing Rob's sporting activities – "When I was a boy...Nobody encouraged me to build myself up" (page 26). How would you react to Mr Willison's obsession with physical development if you were Rob? Can you feel any sympathy for Mr Willison? Is he concerned genuinely for Rob or is he desperately compensating for his own past shortcomings? Note his comment on page 30, "Don't spoil my big night".

9 Why did Rob concoct the business of the boxing tournament and why did he pretend to have appendicitis?

10 Do you feel that Mrs Willison over-reacts in her worrying about Rob's boxing? Would *you*, if you were a mother, feel the same way about your son entering the ring? Why does boxing, even though it is not one of the more dangerous sports in terms of numbers of fatalities, arouse strong feelings

of disapproval in many people?

11 *Like "The Life Guard", "Manhood" ends tantalisingly as Mr Willison "put down the telephone, hesitated, then turned and began slowly to climb the stairs" (page 32). A good short story has this invaluable advantage over the novel; it is detailed and explicit in its presentation of a short, crucial period of someone's life, but since it has not the space to resolve all dilemmas it can stimulate the reader's imagination into an extension of action in a way that the novel, with its frequent sense of finality at its close, cannot. Try extending "Manhood" in order to explore the way in which the relationship between Rob and his father might develop as Mr Willison tops the stairs and enters Rob's bedroom.

12 The theme of this short story has attracted other writers and poets. You may find it interesting to contrast the sentiments of two poems concerning "playing the game", Sir Henry Newbolt's "Vitai Lampada" and James Kirkup's "Rugby League Game". More sombre is a poem with a very long title by Leslie Norris, "Elegy for Lyn James, Killed in The Ring at Shoreditch Town Hall, June 16th, 1964" (this can be found in *Stop and Listen*, an anthology of living poets compiled by John Fairfax, Longman 1969). The motives of one Rugby League player in seeking stardom are examined in David Storey's novel, *This Sporting Life* (published in Longman Heritage of Literature series). A cruel ousting of brawn by brains can be found in John Mortimer's television play script, "David and Broccoli", printed in the collection *Conflicting Generations* in Longman Imprint Books.

King Caliban

13 The title of this story is worth considering. Len Weatherhead coins the name, telling Bert that Caliban "was some kind of monster on a desert island, as far as I know. That's the angle to stress, for Fred. The barbaric" (page 49). In Shakespeare's play, *The Tempest*, Caliban was a deformed, ill-natured monster, the son of a witch, wholly without dignity, perhaps because he was permitted no dignity. In what ways does this name for Fred indicate the attitudes of Weatherhead and of the spectators towards the wrestlers?

And in what ways are these attitudes confirmed in the account of the wrestling in the story?

14 Discuss the details in the description of Fred's bout with "Billy Crusher" which seem to emphasise the degrading quality of commercial wrestling as a sport designed to appeal to the basest qualities in its spectators. It is worth comparing this description with the account of the contest between Schmule and Python Macklin at the end of Wolf Mankowitz's novel, *A Kid For Two Farthings*. Here the victory of Schmule is a happy event for the young boy, Joe, and Wolf Mankowitz makes sure that the behaviour of the crowd and, indeed, the contest itself, is mildly comic. He suppresses the disturbing undertones. John Wain does not hide his concern. Where is John Wain's concern most evident in this story?

15 How much do you blame Bert individually for the tragic mistake of putting Fred in the wrestling ring? To what extent is Doreen's attitude responsible for Bert's putting the plan into action? What indications are there in the story that John Wain is putting the blame in part on the attitudes of an acquisitive, materialistic society? (Bert speaks feelingly to Fred of "the time when the kids were teen-agers and needed all sorts of things to help them keep up with the crowd – smart clothes and motor-scooters and the rest of it" – page 42).

16 The story of Fred explores the theme of the potentially frightening combination of low intelligence with great physical strength. It is a disturbing moment in Bert's narrative when he recalls that after Arthur had slammed Fred in the kidneys with his fist after the practice bout Bert "didn't like the look in his eyes. ...All of his gentleness was gone..." (page 48). Is it this fear of an uncontrollable outburst of physical violence that is responsible for society's failure to allow human dignity to the physically strong but mentally weak Fred's of this world? For another poignant story on this theme you should read John Steinbeck's short novel *Of Mice and Men,* the story of a pathetic and lovable but mentally retarded strong man, Lennie, and the devotion of his friend George, a devotion which fails to protect Lennie from a fatal train of events when he encounters a woman whom George describes as "a jail bait all set on the trigger".

17 Discuss the ways in which we are able to learn more about Bert as a person by having him tell the story for himself. How does the use of a first person narrative technique in story-writing enable an author to project his own feelings towards the principal characters by a process of self-revelation by the narrator? Look at other stories which make use of first person narrative, Alan Sillitoe's novel *Saturday Night and Sunday Morning*, for instance.

18* To test whether first person narrative can, in certain circumstances, bring writer and reader into more intimate contact, see the suggestions for the extensions of the stories "The Life Guard" and "Manhood" (points 6 and 11). Write Jimmy's *own* story of events after the tragedy or Rob's *own* story of what happened after his father discovered the boxing tournament hoax.

I Love You, Ricky

19 John Wain writes of the girls being "equally inflamed by Ricky's rooster-performance" (page 57). What do you think he is implying in his use of the phrase "rooster-performance"? Is it a fair implication and do you think the phrase can be used in describing male pop stars today?

20 Are the feelings of Hilda and Elizabeth towards Ricky's cufflink typical of any pop fans today? Have you acquired any similar souvenirs from pop concerts you have attended, or do you know of any friends who have? If so, what have the souvenirs meant to you or to your friends?

21 Have a look at the passage which describes Hilda's pleasure in listening to Ricky's records in her room and which compares Elizabeth's "essential vulgarity" in having many of Ricky's photographs plastered on her wall with Hilda's "worship" of "one big glossy picture" ("Meanwhile, under her mask of penitence...for his sake", page 61). Do you find Hilda's behaviour in any way typical of that of teenage girls who idolise a male pop star? Hilda classifies her feeling as "worship". Can you analyse her feelings more realistically? How essential are the photographs in the magazines, the posters for the walls, in fact all the *visual* accompaniments of a passion for a particular pop star? What precisely do these accompaniments add to enthusiasm?

22* What differences do you find between the *public* experience of listening to pop music or watching a pop star and the *private* experiences in your own room with the posters, the record sleeves, and the sounds of the music? Try to probe these differences by writing two accounts, one of a disco or a pop concert, the other of your reactions – thoughts and fantasies – when listening alone to records of your favourite pop star or stars.

23 Had *you* been "found out" as Hilda was, would you have reacted in the same way by taking down Ricky's picture and parcelling away his records in a drawer? How would *you* have reacted in this situation?

24 How do you view the behaviour of young Rodney in this story? Is his role in any way similar to that of Agnes, Hopper's young sister in "The Life Guard"? Do you experience any similar problems of lack of sensitivity and understanding in your younger brothers or sisters or in younger children known to you?

25 "No one else knows how to love as I do: utterly, consumingly, daring and sacrificing all" (page 61). So thinks Hilda. What forms would Hilda's passionate attachment have taken before the commercial development of pop music and the cult of the pop star? Try to find out something from any older people known to you of *their* attachments to the great romantic film stars of the 1920s, 1930s and 1940s, from Rudolph Valentino, for instance, to Clark Gable. For them was the darkness of the cinema the private equivalent of your room, the posters and the records? And before that? In the eighteenth century the development of what is termed the epistolary novel (a novel set out as a sequence of letters rather than as a sequence of chapters) was influenced partly by the greater leisure afforded to some women in society, providing them with the opportunity to *read* in privacy the intimate thoughts of characters in a novel.

Christmas at Rillingham's

26 Discuss the qualities in Mr Rillingham which annoyed Sidney. Would Sidney have felt less hostile towards Mr Rillingham if Rillingham had paid less attention to Patty?

Was Sidney jealous at all? Was Rillingham a good business-man, in his motives for encouraging Patty, for instance?

27 Sidney found Rillingham's remark to Patty, "The shop isn't the only one that's going to get a Christmas treat, is it?" (page 70) rather suggestive. From the evidence of the story do you think that Mr Rillingham and Patty were having an affair after hours and that this was why Rillingham was having the answering service installed? Or was Sidney jumping to the wrong conclusions?

28 How does Sidney's behaviour in the shop contrast with his behaviour when he meets the au pair girl, particularly the way in which he gives the impression to the girl that Rillingham's is a really big business concern? How would you explain Sidney's reactions from the point where the au pair girl dials the answering service to the end of the story? During the 1950s, at the time when rock-and-roll and Elvis Presley first appeared on the pop scene, compulsory National Service – two years in the Armed Forces – still faced young men at eighteen. Did this fact affect Sidney's decision to record his own Christmas message in any way?

29* We experience the atmosphere of Rillingham's in the rock-and-roll era of the 1950s. What changes would Sidney find in today's record shops? In what ways do record producers and record shop owners add to the temptation to buy records? Write your impressions of a record shop or department known to you now, describing the staff, the customers, and the overall atmosphere.

30* Would Mr Rillingham be capable of owning and managing a present-day record shop? Try a rewrite of "Christmas At Rillingham's" twenty or more years on from the Christmas of this story. In your rewrite try to provide Rillingham's with up-to-date staff. How would a substitute "Patty" turn out?

31 Although it obviously annoys Sidney, Rillingham's often repeated statement, "It's the young people today, in the world we're living in, that have got the money" is an important cornerstone of his business philosophy, and from the evidence of the story it seems to be paying off. Do you think that his statement still holds good today? To what extent

do you think that record sales to young people are boosted by the presence of the "charts" and of the constant references to the charts by radio disc jockeys?

32 What would you consider to be John Wain's own feelings about Mr Rillingham, Sidney, and Patty, from the way in which he tells the story? And what would appear to be his feelings about the world of pop in the two stories, "I Love You Ricky" and "Christmas At Rillingham's"?

Rafferty

33 In what ways do you find the social level of this story very different from the social levels of the stories in this collection so far? How, for instance, do you think that the Willisons in "Manhood" would react to the social world of Isobel and Walter? How would Sidney, in "Christmas At Rillingham's", cope?

34 Discuss how Rafferty comes to dominate the story, even though he only appears late in the story and then he doesn't speak.

35 Would you feel the same about Rafferty if you were Walter? Why does Walter persist in talking about Rafferty when he is with Isobel? What do you make of Walter's behaviour at the party? Why did he go to the party with Isobel?

36 What are the dangers of any relationship which starts when either the man or the woman is "on the rebound"? What was it about Rafferty which made such a big impression on Isobel? Has Isobel really recovered from her affair with Rafferty? Does Walter believe she has? Is Isobel merely being cautious towards Walter or is she not really interested in him? What do her final words, "It was fun, it was fun, it was fun" (page 89) suggest about her attitude to the evening and about her possible future with Walter? Can you see any future for Isobel and Walter?

37* Write (if you've experienced it) your own account of the experience of being "on the rebound". Or, alternatively, if you have met a young man who has had a similar impact to that of Rafferty on Isobel or you have met a young woman who has had a similar impact to that of Isobel on Walter, try to describe the impact and the events surrounding it.

38* Discuss the special atmospheres of various types of parties. What do parties reveal of human relationships and what do they sometimes expose of human weaknesses? Write an account of a party you have been to, concentrating on the ways in which guests reveal unexpected sides of their characters and react in unexpected ways.

39 What special interest and what possible value is there in reading literature which deals with social, historical, or geographical environments in complete contrast to those of the reader? Talk about examples of this kind of reading experience.

40 After reading "Rafferty" consider the ways in which atmosphere and tension can be built up in a short story by the almost exclusive use of dialogue with a minimum of explanatory description or narrative.

The Valentine Generation

41 Discuss the separate arguments put forward by the postman and by the girl in this story. Whose arguments do you find the more convincing? Does the generation gap existing between the two make it easier or harder for the postman to break the regulations in the end and to give the girl her letter? "Everything's different with you young people today," claims the postman. (page 92) "You belong to a different generation," accuses the girl. (page 97) But just how different are the girl's thoughts about love from those of the postman? How different are your thoughts on love from those of your parents?

42* How would a postman the same age as the girl have reacted to her request, do you think? Try to write the dialogue which might have taken place between the girl and a young postman.

43 What do we learn about the postman and his attitude both to his job and to his life, as a direct consequence of John Wain's having him tell the story for himself? (See also point no. 17, referring to "King Caliban", page 134.)

44* People are often prepared to discuss major emotional problems and hang-ups with complete strangers, and the discussion between the postman and the girl is a good example
of this. Why should this be so? Have you had any comparable
experiences of discussing the intimate details of your life
with relative strangers and if so could you write about the
circumstances surrounding the occasion? Alternatively, perhaps you could write about times of crisis in your life when
it has been easier to talk with a close friend than with a
close relative.

45* John Wain has created a tense and entertaining story here
from a situation which most people must have feared at
some time in their lives: what do you do if you post a letter
and then realise that you should never have written the
letter! Discuss other situations where the posting of a letter
could have drastic results. You might write a story exploring
a situation where a letter that you regret posting actually
goes on its way and is delivered.

46 Why does the postman take the regulations so seriously?
Why is this particular regulation vitally necessary? Discuss
other jobs in which regulations which at first might seem
harshly inflexible are necessary for the wider protection of
the public – regulations on the railway, for instance.

47 "I wonder what May'd say. Not that I'll ever know. There
are some things a man keeps to himself" (page 99). Would
you go home and tell your wife of an incident like this, or
would you keep the incident to yourself? Is the postman's
attitude here that of a different generation? Are young
people less worried at the prospect of recounting such in-
cidents to husbands or wives, boyfriends or girlfriends?

A Message from the Pig-man

48 In its terse, poignant few pages this story pinpoints harshly
the problems of a young child's even beginning to understand
why his father should leave home, to be replaced by another
man. For Ekky it seemed "mad and pointless that Donald's
coming should mean that Dad had to go" (page 101). Discuss
the problems raised for a young child by the break-up of
his parents' marriage. What other problems will Ekky have
to face? What kind of questions will Ekky be putting to

Donald? Or will his mother's and Donald's failure to answer the question, "Why can't Dad be with us even if Donald *is* here?" mean that Ekky will tend to withdraw into himself instead?

49 The Pig-Man must surely have had his equivalent figure in the minds of most children – the local eccentric character, perhaps rather elderly, perhaps rather strangely dressed, the living image of one's shadowy fears of the bogey-man out to catch one and carry one off. Discuss characters who similarly frightened you as a small child. What did you find frightening and what kind of fantasies did you weave in your mind about them?

√50 Why, for Ekky, was his actual meeting with the Pig-Man so important in the circumstances? The story is entitled "A Message from the Pig-Man", but the message wasn't direct, only implied. What precisely *was* the implied message for Ekky and how did he act upon it? And how did the result of his acting upon it affect his state of mind?

51* Write a story entitled "The Question" in which you recall an occasion in your own childhood or adolescence when you felt compelled to ask a vitally important question, one as important as the question Ekky put to his mother. Describe the circumstances leading up to the question, explain whether you actually put the question or not, and describe the aftermath.

52* Write an open letter to parents with young children who are contemplating separation or divorce, in which you warn them of the sort of effects their actions may have on their children's present and future behaviour and attitudes.

Down Our Way

53 In his misuse of the Christian religion to feed his own personal bigotry and intolerance, Mr Robinson is by no means an unusual figure. Discuss the dangers of Mr Robinson's literal interpretations of the Bible as a basis for making the Bible imply just whatever it suits Mr Robinson to make it imply. Why has this essentially tolerant Christian religion produced so much intolerance and suffering over the past two thousand years?

54 What effects has Mr Robinson's personal brand of Christianity had on the attitudes of the members of his family? Discuss the irony of Mr Major's producing of the photographs from his wallet. What does John Wain wish to emphasise by his inclusion of this small but significant incident in his story?

55 This story is, quite deliberately, an unpleasant revelation of racial prejudice. To what extent can literature exert an influence towards the reduction of racial prejudice? Many writers have produced some of their finest work because of a sense of commitment to write about social injustices. You might be interested to read Alan Paton's two novels concerned with racial problems in South Africa, *Cry The Beloved Country* and *Too Late the Phalarope*. On the other hand, can television comedy series designed principally for entertainment rather than for the serious encouragement of toleration really help? Or do they only in the long term perpetuate racial fun-poking and, thus, intolerance?

56* Try to write the sequel to this story – Mr Major's own account of his experiences after he has moved in as a lodger with the Robinson family. Bear in mind Mrs Robinson's comment, "He'll soon put a foot wrong and as soon as he does I'll have him out" (page 115).

57 Discuss this type of setting for stories, stories not necessarily connected with racial intolerance but rather stories exploring the claustrophobic tensions of urban families in densely populated urban streets. Why and to what extent do such urban environments breed intolerance and even violence? You can find plenty of use of such settings in short stories by Stan Barstow and Alan Sillitoe. You might also consider the effects of urban environment on the attitudes of pupils and parents towards a coloured teacher in E.R. Braithwaite's autobiographical book, *To Sir, With Love*.

58 It is obvious that the Robinsons need the money from letting a room to a lodger; Doris reveals that they've "been advertising in their front window with a room to let for the last six months" (page 108). In what ways can the presence of a lodger, regardless of colour or creed, be a potential source of tension in a household? Discuss the difficulties involved in having a lodger and suggest ways in which they can be lessened or removed.

Goodnight, Old Daisy

59 As well as its highly evocative railway theme this story also develops a theme which is constantly full of a disturbing pathos: the awareness on the part of the elderly of the thinly or clumsily veiled hostility of the young towards them in certain circumstances. What signs of this hostility emerge in this story? How do you regard Cyril Foster's attitude towards the imminent death of his father-in-law at the end of the story? Discuss realistically some of the problems of having an elderly relative living in a small house which contains children. How can the possible frictions be reduced or removed?

60 In what ways do the pressures of this last day in Mr Greeley's life build up, possibly contributing directly to his death? Do events suggest that Mr Greeley could be rather difficult to communicate with? Is he too sensitive to change, or is this characteristic of old age?

61* Memories and the resultant nostalgia for the past play a major part in the daily thought-routines of many elderly people. For men these thoughts are often related to the job they had until retirement, particularly if, as in Mr Greeley's case, the job has had a great appeal to the imagination. Discuss some of the careers which seem particularly prone to producing nostalgia in the elderly, service in the Forces, or a lifetime in the entertainment world, for instance. Consider, too, the use made by the broadcasting media of the entertainment value of reminiscence. Good reminiscences are not the exclusive province of the well-known. Try to unlock the memories of some elderly people known to you and either tape them or adapt them into a first-person piece of nostalgic writing.

62* The tremendous sense of atmosphere generated in this story comes from the very special appeal of the steam locomotive. The enthusiasm for the days of steam continues unabated and Mr Greeley, were he alive now, would probably find that many young boys and young men unable to remember steam days are fascinated by the surviving steam lines operated by enthusiasts, by the ever-increasing books and magazines devoted to steam, and by the considerable discography of steam locomotive sounds in existence. Discuss the reasons for this continued enthusiasm. Your discussions will be aided if, for instance, you can get hold of some copies of the monthly magazine *Railway World* (Ian Allen publications), or can listen to a recording of the radio ballad, "The Ballad of John Axon" (Argo Records) and to some of the superb Argo Transacord recordings of steam locomotives in action (" 'Newfoundland' Heads 'The Waverley' " is an ideal recording to listen to in relation to this story). Finally, try to sum up the whole theme in a written discussion of "The Appeal of Steam".

63 John Wain vividly brings alive the footplate sensations of the past in the final dream sequence of Mr Greeley's trip on "Old Daisy". How does he re-create the precise sensations? Look carefully at the details in this account, the technical terms, the words describing sounds and movements, the details recreating the landscape as it was in Mr Greeley's heyday before modern development had altered it.

Other Writing by John Wain

Novels

John Wain has reached his widest reading public through his novels. It would probably be fair to say that since the mid-1950s John Wain has been and still is one of the more significant contemporary English novelists. Perhaps the best books to start with are *Hurry On Down* and *Strike the Father Dead*.

Hurry On Down

This was John Wain's first novel, published in 1953. Its principal character, Charles Lumley, is anti-heroic in conception. As such, he is an early example of an important trend in the provincial novels of the late 1950s and early 1960s, the presentation of young, abrasive, regional characters in mildly unsuccessful revolt against various aspects of society. We meet such characters in Kingsley Amis's *Lucky Jim*, Alan Sillitoe's *Saturday Night and Sunday Morning*, Keith Waterhouse's *Billy Liar* and David Storey's *This Sporting Life*.

Charles Lumley, at the beginning of *Hurry On Down*, has just come down from the university with a mediocre degree in History. He has no job and no prospects, claiming that "the University had, by its three years' random and shapeless cramming, unfitted his mind for serious thinking". But his attitudes and his situation are not produced by any perverse intention to become a drop-out. They are, rather, a reflection of a fear that he has been processed, by both school and university education, into a middle-class professional product. "He hated his own kind", yet "he was imprisoned in his class". His dilemma is pinpointed when, after taking up window-cleaning, he returns to his old school and suggests to his old headmaster that he should be given a contract to clean the school windows. The headmaster regards his suggestion as "a foolish joke" and rings the bell for the janitor to escort him off the premises. Soon afterwards, Charles Lumley comes into contact with an old undergraduate acquaintance, Edwin Froulish, an eccentric who is living with his mistress in a loft, forming part of a derelict builder's yard, whilst he writes "The Novel". Lumley moves in with them, and during his stay he accompanies them to a meeting of the Stotwell Literary Society, the President of which is another old student of Lumley's university, June Veebers. John Wain's account of this meeting is a delicious send-up, not just of the experimental writer but of the rather precious characters who have been known to frequent Literary Societies:

"And so, for our first meeting of the winter session," said June Veeber's bell-like voice, making the words sound like an invitation to some kind of orgy, "we welcome Mr Froulish, who will read extracts from his Work in Progress."

She sat down. George Hutchins jammed his chair against hers and surreptitiously took her hand under cover of a newspaper.

Froulish leaned forward, his face a blind, twitching mask. He jerked his arm and knocked over his glass in a gesture so unnatural it must surely have been intentional – yet for that very reason Charles put it down to genuine nervousness.

Everyone waited for him to speak. He stared at them, fingering the top sheet of his pile of typescript, jerking his left leg spasmodically. A man cleared his throat with a noise like a cavalry carbine being fired in a railway tunnel. It was the society's bore: Mr Gunning-Forbes, senior English master at the local grammar school. Charles had once cleaned his windows.

"Ladies and gentlemen," Froulish whispered hoarsely. Smoke began to curl upwards from where he had dropped his cigarette on to the hearthrug. Hutchins moved forward officiously and stamped on the smouldering patch.

"I'll start without any preamble by reading the opening paragraphs of the work."

"What's the title of your book?" demanded Gunning-Forbes suspiciously, resting his hands on the stained knees of his flannels.

"No title," said Froulish impatiently. "Just a dark blue binding. No lettering, no title-page."

"What's the idea of that?" growled the schoolmaster, with increased hostility. "Thought becomes impossible if things haven't got names. Thought, in fact, consists – "

"I should have thought it was obvious," cried Froulish passionately. "I should have thought it was axiomatic. No title – impossible to give in a few words any idea of what it's about. About things that can't be put in a nutshell. About human life. Just a book – you want to know what it says, you read it and find out. Resisting the idea that things of any importance can be labelled and fitted into categories."

Gunning-Forbes was on his feet, but June Veeber leaned across and put her hand on his sleeve. He turned and stared at her, then slowly sat down, his steel-rimmed spectacles flashing grimly.

"First few paragraphs," said Froulish, taking off his collar and tie and throwing them into the fire – surely a contrived effect, but impossible to be certain. "Nothing to do with the actual action of the book. Just a melodic and oblique stroke or semantic preparation."

"Say that again," rapped out Gunning-Forbes.

"I said," Froulish repeated, "a melodic and oblique stroke or semantic preparation." There was a silence.

"A king ringed with slings," began Froulish without more ado, "a thing without wings but brings strings and sings. Ho, the slow foe! Show me the crow toe I know, a beech root on the beach, fruit of a rich bitch, loot in a ditch, shoot a witch, which foot?"

Hutchins stirred uneasily in his seat.

"Clout bell, shout well, pell-mell about a tout, get the hell out. About nowt. Court log wart hog bought a dog."

Gunning-Forbes's glasses sparkled with fury. The schoolteachers and bank clerks stared in bewilderment. Hutchins caught June Veeber's eye and smiled lasciviously. Charles took deep breaths of cigarette smoke. Froulish droned on.

"Deep in the grass, a cheap farce, glass weeps for Tom Thumb, a bum's dumb chum. That's the end of that part," Froulish concluded. His audience returned to life. Drooping heads came upright.

"Well, if that's the preamble, what about the story? Why don't you outline the plot?" demanded Gunning-Forbes.

"Outline the what?" sneered Froulish. He seemed itching for a quarrel with the old man.

"The plot. Outline the plot and then read us a few extracts to show how your characters are developed."

"Don't make me laugh, I've got a split lip," said Froulish contemptuously. Opposition had braced his fibres: thanks to its tonic effect he was alert, happy, even gay. Gone was the usual neurotic unrest and gloom; he was a living proof that every man is biologically equipped with marvellous reserves of power to be called on when defending what he really believes in. Charles, from his corner, saw the transformation and was humbled, thinking of Betty's ferocious defence of her mate. So much, so much that he had never guessed at!

"Nevertheless, Mr Froulish," June Veeber cut in frostily, before the brawl could develop any further, "do read us some more. Couldn't you pick some passage that illustrates a central theme or tendency of the book?"

"Now you're talking," replied the novelist, who was quite docile so long as the word "plot" was not uttered. "I'll just explain the central situation. Six people are trapped in a lift between two floors of a skyscraper – a musician, a surgeon, a charwoman, a conjurer and his female assistant, and a hunchback carrying a small suitcase."

"Containing some sandwiches, I hope," chuckled the local curate. "They're bound to get hungry before long."

"You can fill in the details for yourself," said Froulish, not realising that the man imagined himself to be joking. "Where was I? Yes, these six are in the lift. Part of the book consists of a series of flashbacks, every one twice the length of the average novel, over the previous life of each of them. Not their physical lives, just the psychic currents that flowed through them. It's expressed chiefly through patterns of imagery."

"God help us," said Gunning-Forbes loudly.

"Meanwhile," Froulish went on, "they're trying to send a message to the chief electrician, who lives in the basement, to do something about getting the lift going. At least, there's a door marked 'Chief Electrician', but no one's ever seen it open or seen anyone go in or out. Messages have to be written in a ritual code and slipped under the door."

Gunning-Forbes had begun to take an interest. "Not a bad touch that," he commented. "Illustrate the way the working classes have got above themselves since the war, eh?"

Fortunately Froulish ignored him.

"They don't seem to be able to get a message through. At first they pass the time trying to keep cheerful. The conjurer draws billiard-balls out of the musician's ears, the surgeon diagnoses everyone's physical condition and says what operations he recommends, the charwoman sings Edwardian music-hall songs. The hunchback is the only one who doesn't do anything. He doesn't speak either."

"Doesn't seem much point in having him there," from Gunning-Forbes.

"A couple of days pass, and gradually they're being driven mad with hunger and thirst. Finally, when they're in the last stages of exhaustion and despair, the hunchback offers to put them out of their misery. He takes a hand-grenade out of his suitcase. Exploding in that confined space it's quite enough to kill them all. Then they have a long debate as to who shall pull the pin out to make the thing go off. There's a theological point there, among others. The one who does it will be guilty of both suicide and murder."

He paused. His audience looked at him apathetically. Betty's eyes never wavered from June Veeber's face.

"Finally the conjurer comes to their aid. He conjures it out. Makes it jump out without seeming to touch it. Before he could be shown to be guilty of suicide, it would be necessary to prove that he'd touched the pin, and that's not possible."

"Oh come," cried the curate from the back row. Froulish in his stride, ignored him.

"Anyway, now they're all dead. The blast frees the lift, and it drops down to the ground floor. So the corpses are taken out. Naturally, in laying them out, any papers they have about them are removed and studied to help in identification. That's how they find out," he paused dramatically, "that the hunchback was the Chief Electrician."

There was a silence.

"Well, go on," said Gunning-Forbes encouragingly.

"That's the end," scowled Froulish.

There was a scraping of chairs.

"So that's your plot, is it?" said Gunning-Forbes judicially. "D'you want to know what I think of it?"

"No, but you evidently want to tell me."

"I think it's got the makings of a fairly good yarn, provided of course that you cut out this verbal tomfoolery and make it clean-cut. Except for one bad flaw."

He waited for Froulish to ask what that was, but the novelist was rolling himself a cigarette and showed no sign of hearing, so he went on.

"That man wouldn't have had a hand-grenade in his suitcase. People don't. It's just not true to life."

"Couldn't he have been a traveller for a firm that made hand-grenades?" asked the curate. Charles wondered whether he was mad or just drunk.

"Not possible," Gunning-Forbes shook his head. "He was supposed to be the Chief Electrician. He couldn't have combined the two jobs. No good novelist would bring in anything as far-fetched as that. A course of Thackeray, that's my prescription –

soon weed out these little faults. Then you might make some real headway."

He sat back benevolently. Froulish flushed scarlet. He began to sway backwards and forwards in his chair, feverishly flicking his short fingers; the usual sign that he was violently agitated. Charles held his breath for the outburst. But he was forestalled.

Hutchins had hitherto been mercifully silent, dividing his energies between fawning on the thickset siren beside him and looking superciliously round the room, but now he decided, evidently, that the time had come for him to put on his act and dazzle the company. He took out a pipe and filled it. Charles could see from the light colour and stringy texture of the tobacco that it was some kind of very mild mixture; he was not surprised, for Hutchins, though needing a pipe for the successful acting of his part, was handicapped by a weak stomach. Even now he did not light the pipe, but stuck it in his mouth, pulled it out again, twiddled it in his fingers, and finally jammed it between his front teeth and spoke in an exaggeratedly precise, high-pitched voice.

"I suppose, Froulish, that what you're doing there is something that might be described by an ordinary chap like me – " he smiled boyishly, to show that they were not to believe him – "as a return to allegory. Would you place yourself in a direct line of descent from Kafka?"

He waited for Froulish's reply with the calm, condescending air of a man who is accustomed to examining ideas and putting them in order, but is nevertheless prepared to have patience with those who habitually leave a mass of tangled loose ends. The young scholar doing a little intellectual slumming.

"No," replied Froulish shortly. "My masters are Dante, Spinoza, Rimbaud, Boehme, and Grieg."

Hutchins champed agitatedly on his pipestem. His face lost a little of its buoyant expression; he was not sure whether his leg was being pulled, and it was important for him, having entered the lists under the eye of his lady, to come off best.

"Grieg, now that's a very interesting point," he said. He pointed at Froulish with his pipe. "What made you put a musician into a list composed otherwise of writers? You may think it's only a small point" ("Not a point at all," from Gunning-Forbes) "but what we're all interested in here, is how the minds of chaps like you work. Our own minds," he smiled again to indicate that they need not think he meant all their minds were as good as his, "work by the ordinary methods, travel by, I think

I could say, the ordinary routes. But chaps like you seem to have discovered, er," he did not want to say short cuts, it sounded too trite, so ended, "short-circuits." Hell, that was wrong. Short-circuits was wrong.

Froulish told Charles afterwards that he had been on the point of replying, "I refer, of course to Aloysius Grieg, the seventeenth-century Abbot of Helsingfors, author of the Tractatus Virorum et Angelorum, and particularly to the spurious third book", but in fact, he contented himself with saying stiffly, "Of course, I didn't expect everyone to pick that point up, though I expect most people would see it all right. I mean, of course, Grieg's tone colours, and particularly his handling of the woodwind. I regard the vowels 'e' and 'u' as the woodwinds of the verbal orchestra, and an accurate count would reveal, as you doubtless noticed, that they predominate over the rest in what I might call the slow movements of my work."

Hutchins summoned all his dwindling reserves. June Veeber was looking at him in a way that did not help much.

"Well, no, I can't say I did notice," he said, jolly and aggressive, the manner of the don when he tells you he does not understand something so as to convey that he thinks you a fool for pretending you do, "you chaps do tend to give the rest of us credit for perceptions about your work that we don't, I think, always have." He looked round the room for support, but they stared at him stonily; the discussion had gone on too long. "Was that, for instance, the bit you read us just now – was that a slow movement?"

"No," said Froulish calmly. "It was a cadenza."

Meeting Hutchins's bewildered gaze, he stared at him triumphantly, at the same time taking out a pocket comb and running it through his hair. A shower of dandruff was plainly visible under the electric light.

June Veeber rose. She was determined, evidently, to end the proceedings before the society should be permanently crippled. Besides, she wanted to get George Hutchins by himself and give him a few remarks on making a fool of himself in public. June's young men were kept up to the mark.

"Coffee will be served in a few minutes – Miss Wotherspoon, would you be frightfully kind and do your usual? Thank you so much." Miss Wotherspoon's "usual" was to trudge down to the school kitchen, make the coffee, and carry it up. "And meanwhile I'm sure we all thank Mr Froulish very much for a most stimulating evening, and we look forward with great interest to the time when his book will be published."

"You look forward a damn long time, then," returned Froulish curtly. "This is only the first draft. The thing probably won't be finished for fifteen years. My name isn't – Trollope."

He pronounced the last word with so much deliberation, and looked so fixedly at June Veeber, that Charles could have sworn the insult was intentional. His feeling seemed to be shared; startled by a sudden low neighing sound, he looked round. Betty was laughing.

Strike the Father Dead

This novel was published in 1962. Jeremy Coleman, fond of jazz and becoming increasingly hostile to the disapproval of his father who is Professor of Classics at a provincial university, runs away from school and home in 1942 and goes to wartime London to try his luck as a jazz pianist. The story is told by three people – Alfred (Jeremy's father), Eleanor (Alfred's sister), and Jeremy himself. This narrative technique enables the reader to view Jeremy's adventures from three different standpoints. It particularly helps us to see the way in which Professor Coleman's dour academic outlook makes him intolerant of his son's natural antipathy to "the eternal Greek grammar" and incapable of understanding that Jeremy could find an aesthetic fulfilment in the art of jazz. Reading this novel after reading *Hurry On Down* one could well imagine Professor Coleman and his fellow academics producing the environment which triggered off the revolt of Charles Lumley.

Jeremy Coleman leads a chequered existence, first in London, then, for a time later, in Paris. But, helped by his close friendship with a brilliant Negro jazz musician, Percy, he maintains an artistic integrity of purpose, single-mindedly devoted to jazz, refusing to be corrupted by commercial trends. This integrity of purpose is well illustrated in an episode towards the end of the novel. Jeremy describes the first date of the newly constituted Jeremy Coleman Band. It was an engagement as supporting band at a big ballroom, the Athenaeum, in a London suburb. The main band was, as Jeremy puts it, "a rock-and-roll outfit, currently much in the news, called by some tomfool made-up name, Rod Tempest and his Lightning Conductors or some such". In this episode John Wain, through Jeremy's narrative, enables us to take a humorous but ironic look at commercial "pop" music of the rock-and-roll era of the 1950s. The implications remain highly relevant in the 1970s.

If the noise outside had been loud, inside it was insane. Rod Tempest and his boys were up on the stand, thrashing like eels and pounding on their instruments. The members of the band were dressed in a uniform that vaguely suggested the open air – check shirts with the sleeves rolled up, and that kind of thing. Rod Tempest himself, the big man, was dressed from head to foot in white, with a big white cowboy hat on his head. I'd heard of him of course: he wasn't exactly a singer, nor exactly a player: he just projected his personality out in front of the band, and yelled the words of whatever they were playing. He was just cutting loose as we went in, swaying about and flapping his hands, with his back to the band. A solid wall of noise behind him and hundreds of excited kids in front. He was yelling out one of those simplified refrains that rock-and-rollers go in for. I remember one couplet of it:

> Hail, hail,
> Rock an' roll;
> Deliver me
> From days of old.

The kids were shouting the refrain with him – at least some were, and the rest were just screaming aimlessly, like animals trapped in a burning arena. I just stood there with Percy and we looked. First at the band, with this big phony slob in his white suit gyrating up and down, then at the kids in their jeans, check shirts and jerseys, hopping up and down with excitement and bawling.

I caught Percy's eye and made a gesture of despair. If this moron could sweep them off their feet, how could they possibly like what we were going to give them? Percy understood my gesture, bent over and put his ear to my mouth, and uttered the one word, "Cool". That made me laugh and broke the evil spell. "Cool." That's the word every one of these kids would use to describe the noise made by that sweating, pounding mob on the stand. It was their term of praise. It meant anything that conformed to the values of their world, the one they had created out of their own needs and preferences. And I didn't grudge it to them. In the world of popular entertainment these adolescents had the adults in their power. They were in a position to dictate, to say what they wanted and get it.

But, Christ! That *this* should be the result! Of course, I reflected as I watched Rod Tempest break out into a final flurry of stamping and bawling, it had to come. Popular music is like journalism. If a chap takes your customers away by appealing to a lower taste, you have to get them back by appealing to a lower one still. The advantage will always be with the one who can dive lowest – till, finally, you both get to rock-bottom and stay there. This stuff, Rod Tempest and the like, was rock-bottom. You took jazz and simplified it. Having discovered that what the average adolescent likes about jazz is its rhythm, you stepped up the rhythm and cut down the melody. Finally you were left with a music that consisted of nine-tenths rhythm and one-tenth melody – the "melody" consisting of a few phrases repeated over and over again in a honking, brawling tone. Any instrument that couldn't hold its own in this atmosphere – the clarinet, for instance – was out. All you needed was a simple alternation of coarse, shouting brass and the kind of saxophone that can be used as part of the rhythm section in between solos. Honk, honk, behind the other soloists. There can't ever have been a simpler music, or one easier to reproduce. Once the formula was arrived at, everybody was in the money.

I walked nearer to the bandstand (as nearly as I could for the press of sweating, clapping fans) and took a closer look at the "musicians". I knew them all; not individually, but as a type. They were the solid, unteachable, bottom layer of the dance-band world. The type who'd become musicians to get out of the machine-shop. Good luck to them. But once they were out, once they'd acquired a saxophone or a trumpet on the never-never, and paid for a series of lessons and turned pro, they'd never realised there was anything else to do. Here they were, with their dull, expressionless faces glittering above their instruments, bashing out the stuff that was put in front of them. Last year it had been saccharine waltzes and "ballads", next year it might be calypso and Afro-Cuban; whatever it was, they would still be there, turning it out without question, taking home a good pay-packet and leaving the arguments to other people. My mind went back to that first night out, when I went to Lucille's flat with those two chaps from the band, Chuck and the other man. Chuck! I recalled him so vividly at that moment, with his characterless face and body, his fake

American accent, and the general stale second-handness that hung about him. Well, these chaps were all like Chuck. Someone had discovered a formula that would suck money out of these youngsters' pockets, and the Chucks of this world had all been signed on to do their share of the sucking.

> Hail, hail,
> Rock an' roll:
> Deliver me
> From days of old,

the kids sang as they hopped about. To me, at thirty-three, they looked as alike as tadpoles. Just so many conditioned reflexes, ready to respond to a deft tap on the right spot. Not that "deft tap" is the right description of what Rod and his myrmidons were doing. They were hammering away like drunken blacksmiths. BAM-tiddy-BAM-tiddy-BAM-tiddy-BAM, on and on without the least variation, the least imagination, till I thought I'd go mad. As for the kids, they *had* gone mad, long ago. Their eyes were glassy and they were jigging about like stick-insects. I had a sudden vision of all those knee-joints bending and straightening, all those ankles flexing, all those elbows swaying in and out: it was like watching a giant machine, thousands of ball-and-socket mechanisms all working perfectly, oiled with sweat and money. So Chuck and his friends thought they were getting away from the machine-shop! And here they were, stuck in the middle of a huge assembly-line!

Rod and his Chucks were just about due to come down off the stand and give someone else a chance, but for good measure they went into one last chorus, really churning it up. I turned away – I simply couldn't stand the sight of old Rod in his white suit and cowboy hat another second – and as I did so my eye fell on the couple who happened to be jigging away nearest me. They were dancing on about four square inches of ground, not moving along with the general stream, so I could observe them as closely as if I had been jammed against them in a bus queue in rush hour. They looked about fifteen years old, though I'd better allow for my senility and call it eighteen or nineteen. She was dressed entirely in black; shirt, slacks and shoes all of the same colour. Her hair was black, too, and it was cut in a short boyish crop that emphasised the epicene quality of her face and body. There was nothing feminine about her, any more than there was anything masculine about the boy. I don't, as it happens, remember anything about his appearance at all – he was just a jumping smudge on the fringe of my consciousness. But what struck me about both of this pair was that I simply didn't understand them. I had no clue whatsoever to their feelings or motives. And me, a jazz player. Spending my life making music that young couples like to dance to. I couldn't even tell if there was any sex going on or not. From the peculiar strutting dance they were doing, you might have taken them for a couple of cormorants doing a mating ritual. But the deadness of their faces, and the machine-like air of the whole proceeding, seemed to kill any sexual suggestion. You just couldn't tell – at least I couldn't – whether they were just waiting for the intermission to go round the corner and find a quiet place for a real healthy bash, or whether this was what they did instead.

Rod and his bods finished up by tearing the strings out of the piano, breaking the saxophones in two, stamping on the brass, putting their feet through the drums, sawing the double bass into fragments and finally taking an axe to the platform and setting light to the decorations. The noise must have been audible for twenty miles. I'll give them that, they were paid to make a row and make one they did. Finally the echoes died away and old Rod approached the edge of the platform waving his clasped hands above his head and shouting some kind of slogan. All the kids took it up, and amid a storm of cheers and chanting the band trooped off the platform and disappeared, with Rod fending off the autograph hunters by shouting that they'd be back later and not to worry. So now at last it was our turn.

Some kind of scruffy M.C. went up and said into the mike that he had pleasure in introducing Jeremy Coleman and his band, and we got up there to the accompaniment of a good round of applause. The kids were still in an excited, self-approving state, and they were ready to enjoy another blast of sound. For a moment I half toyed with the idea of asking the boys to give them what they wanted. Step up the rhythm, keep it simplified, stick to riffs and play them good and loud. But the idea died before it was half-way born. In the first place none of us wanted to play like that, and we were all in jazz because it was what we *wanted* to play. In the second place, we couldn't have competed with a mob like Rod's on the noise side. We'd spent years training ourselves to do something more than just kick up a racket, and it was too late to untrain ourselves now, even if our lives had depended on it. Which, of course, they didn't. So I just nodded to the lads and played a few introductory chords and off we went, into a nice medium-tempo twelve-bar blues, which is what we usually started with. Relaxed, but with a nice driving rhythm.

It was going well, I could hear that at once. Percy was playing beautifully: he was gentle, but with a kind of insistence that made his playing very exciting. I began to get ideas, just listening to him, and by the time my solo came round I could just feel the notes forming themselves under my fingers. It was the old champagne: joy, sheer joy. Ted was fizzing away on the drums just to one side of me and the bass player was walking up and down my arteries. "Light, light," I kept thinking. "Light as an invisible feather, light as a bird's breathing." I forgot all about where we were, all about the kids and Rod's mob and the dusty little dressing-room. This was jazz, and I liked it.

The number ended with everyone putting in exactly what was wanted, so that it turned out on to the plate as neatly as a soufflé. We pinned the edges down with one single deft movement, all eight of us working as one, and then sat back with a sigh. It wasn't until five seconds later that we realised that something unusual was happening. What was it? Then we realised. No applause.

At least, I won't say "none". Some of the kids clapped good-naturedly, and others just out of habit. But most of them just stood there and looked at us. Just the same look they'd have given us if we'd played them "Annie Laurie" or "The Bees Wedding".

"Not biting much, are they?" I asked Percy.

He grinned. "They've got no bite left, man," he said easily. "Let's play some music."

I grinned back at him and turned to the keyboard. All the same, some of the snap had gone out of us. Ted picked up his brushes with just a hint of petulance. Like most drummers, he relies very much on come-back from the audience; he has to get them moving with him, or he feels like a man pushing a wagon up a steep hill. I was afraid he'd start trying to get them with him by sheer noise and monotony, like the yokel Rod was employing. And perhaps he would have been willing to, with his conscious mind. But I needn't have worried, of course. He was a good jazzman, who'd been at it as long as I had, and he simply couldn't go back to ham-handed banging. He knew how to build up rhythm unobtrusively, without making a noise, and once you know that you can't go back on it.

That, in a word, was our trouble. We were all too old to get with this rock-and-roll, and, having just heard what Rod's mob were turning out, I was glad to know it. I kept wondering what would have happened if I'd been exposed to that kind of stuff when I was sixteen. Would I have thought it was the thing to imitate? If so, could I possibly have used it as a starting-point? – Could I, that is, have started where Rod's stuff left off? I doubt it, really. The stuff doesn't leave off. It just goes round in a circle, with no way out. I suppose that's why there aren't any jazzmen like Percy and me coming up. The new crop, where they're not just rock-and-rollers, are all conservatory-trained musicians who don't recognise anything as jazz unless it's so abstruse that you've got to be a Beethoven to comprehend it. It makes me glad I grew up when I did, and no later.

We played another couple of numbers, during the course of which most of the kids wandered off to get bottles of Coca-Cola, or something. (It was one of these no-licence, finish-at-eleven-o'clock affairs.) Then, having slaked whatever they have instead of a thirst, they began to drift back and stand about. Waiting for Rod, of course. We were giving them jazz, but they didn't want it. No one was to blame: the agency that booked us ought to have known better, and I'd never have taken the booking if we hadn't been short of dates. But there it was: we'd undertaken to play for a stated length of time, to earn our fee, and we couldn't just step down.

So we played for ourselves. But have you ever tried playing for yourself when there are hundreds of hostile pairs of ears listening and hundreds of voices saying, more or less audibly, that they wished you'd dry up? If you haven't, don't. There's no fun in it. We all began to falter and go dry. All, that is, except Percy. He knew, as well as any of us, what was going on, but he had the gift of being able to climb up into his music and pull the ladder up after him. Listening to him, I marvelled. He was on form, and nobody was going to shake him off it. In the end we all gave up and let Percy carry the whole thing. We just gave him a background, and he went on and on like a bird. I began to enjoy myself again. After all, it wasn't every evening that I had a chance to listen to jazz like this: even from Percy. He was standing beside the piano, with those long arms of his holding the horn at the old tilt, his fingers delicately hopping on the valves, and it was like old times: old times and new times and any times when there was the real spirit.

Then I became aware of something pressing against us. At first I couldn't tell what it was; then I realised that it was a sound, a dead, heavy sound, coming over in slabs, pushing our music over, flattening it, walking across it with great heavy boots.

Percy stopped playing, and so did the rest of us. I let my hands fall from the keyboard and turned to look at the audience. There they all were, all five hundred of them, standing looking up at us. And they were giving us the slow handclap.

So that was it. I suppose it happens to everybody, once. When you're producing something you know is damned good, and putting everything into it, everything you've learnt and everything you are – and then you find, all of a sudden, that you've been offering it to the wrong people.

The kids went on with the slow handclap. Someone began to chant, "We want Rod!" and the others took it up, raggedly at first, then with one solid voice. We want Rod. Well, have him, chums, have him, I thought. He'll deliver you from days of old, which in this case means Jeremy Coleman and his band.

We stood up and gathered our things together. The clapping and chanting went on and on, but there was no particular hostility in the atmosphere. These were modern young people, not given to standing on old-fashioned ceremony. They were paying, and they wanted their money's worth. To them, we were something as old-fashioned as the crinoline, and they weren't in the mood for antiques.

I went to the microphone. "Thank you, ladies and gentlemen," I said. "We'll make way for some more rock-and-roll. That's all for now. Bless your little pointed heads." And I followed the others off the stand.

As a follow-up one might try *The Contenders* and *A Winter In the Hills*.

The Contenders was published in 1958. Its principal characters, narrator Joe Shaw and "the contenders" – Robert Lamb, artist, and Ned Roper, industrialist – all hail from John Wain's home area, The Potteries in North Staffordshire. As with Charles Lumley, in *Hurry On Down*, and Jeremy Coleman, in *Strike the Father Dead*, education provides a key influence on the development of the characters. Joe Shaw, Robert Lamb and Ned Roper attend the same local grammar school and in his narrative Joe Shaw firmly attributes the rivalry between Lamb and Roper to the spirit of competition engendered there. "From the day our schooldays began, we were taught, implicitly, that every other boy was a potential rival and that we must all get down to the sacred task of outdoing one another...we had, in a word, the perfect training for careerists." As a non-contender holding a modest post as a journalist on the local newspaper, Joe Shaw plots the conflicts in the lives and careers of Lamb and Roper in a sequence of episodes which are sometimes comic, sometimes pathetic, but always ironic in their underlining of the possible dangers of the competitive spirit in education when the urge to contend becomes a flaw rather than a virtue in character.

A Winter In the Hills was published in 1970. Its main character, forty-year-old Roger Furnivall, a philologist by profession, comes to North Wales at the end of the season intending to learn Welsh because of an ambition to get a job in the department of Celtic Studies at the University of Uppsala. (He lusts after Uppsala because "he liked tall, blonde girls with perfect teeth and knew that in Uppsala there were a lot of them about".) But his involvement in Welsh life is far more intense than he anticipates. An encounter with Gareth, the owner-driver of a local bus plying between a mountain village and the local town, brings Roger into contact with the cut-throat and occasionally physically violent competition between Gareth, striving to keep his bus service going, and Dic Sharp, another local transport operator anxious to put Gareth out of business. Roger finds himself helping Gareth as his conductor and becoming more loyal to Gareth in his fight to survive and more deeply implicated in the life of a small Welsh community. *Winter In the Hills* is a most compelling and entertaining novel, in which John Wain reveals his ability to present an authentic view of what is essentially a closed society, a rare and understanding penetration of Welsh life by an English writer.

Poetry

John Wain is also a significant poet. Here, for the new reader, is a brief selection. The first is an extract from a sequence of poems, *Letters to Five Artists*, published in 1969. In the Dedication, John Wain writes: "The individual 'Letters' are, of course, dedicated to those to whom they are addressed. The collection as a whole, inasmuch as the wholeness binds them into a unity and calls something distinct into being is offered, in humility, to the ghost of Django Reinhardt."

Django Reinhardt was perhaps the greatest jazz guitarist of this century. Significantly, one of the artists in this collection is Bill Coleman, jazz trumpeter, and this "Letter" should be of special interest to those who have read or who intend to read John Wain's novel *Strike the Father Dead*. The other artists are Victor Neep, the English artist who lives and works in North Wales, Elizabeth Jennings, the poet, who lives in Oxford, Lee Lubbers, an American artist particularly interested in "junk sculpture", and Anthony Conran, English poet living in North Wales.

Letters to Five Artists contains some of John Wain's most easily accessible poetry. The extract which follows has been chosen, however, because of its referring to the poet's own place of birth. It is from the Introductory Poem, a passage in which John Wain writes about the Stoke-on-Trent area and about his father as a child in 1900.

> Yes, and those streets
> in 1900, a boy of six years
> walking those streets, thin, his clothes
> of the cheapest, nearly worn out
> before he got them: but hot
> incitingly hot, under his feet, the brick
> pavement, for some reason I always imagine
> him in summer narrow feet
> on the hot bricks.
>   Polluted water
> and a towpath with rank
> nettles and grass: the thin boy
> prowls amid jagged tins. Heat
> glares from the blue sky. For some
> reason I see him under that hard

blue sky always, smelling polluted
water, watching the smoke
trail its thick arms across, black on blue,
and the bricks hot.
                    Ah, because
it is my own childhood gives me
my vision of his, the streets were the same
after three decades, the same bricks
held the same heat:
                    I wandered,
more often in summer than winter,
smelt the canal, was hungry like him,
I mean like him in his inner hunger, I longed
to reach out, to live, beyond these hot
bricks and round black kilns. Home!
I never doubted it, my home was hunger,
that hunger my blood had caught
from his hasty blood.
                    I see 1900,
trouble in South Africa, volunteers
marching with silver bands down London Road:
I see the thin boy
hungry
always hungry
for food, for life, for the promise that rises
to his narrow feet from the hot bricks.
Where does the canal go? Who reads the signal
poured across the sky by the fat kilns?
Power, money, and trouble:
Wedgwood and Kruger, Spode
and Smuts.
                    The old queen
turns in her bed and dies. The thin boy,
my father, sees his mother draw the blinds.
The blinds of home. The bailiff has the chairs.
The old queen dies. Grandmother draws the blinds
on the bare dusty room. End of a world.
The kilns go belching on, and Wedgwood is
A liberal M.P.
                    The boy is hungry:
He needs so many kinds of nourishment.
His hunger came to me. I have it still.

Home, home! The narrow houses and the kilns,
The stinking water. The tip above the roofs.
And half a dozen brick town halls.
Why is it always summer in my dream?
Because of the hot sunlight in his eyes?
To speak of exile is to speak of home.
The drumming hoofs across the ice: the poet
listless, far from Rome. Seventy years ago
the smell of the canal and the fat kilns.
The burning arrows crackle in the thatch.
The lost plank floats in the scum-laden water.
The poet shivers. The thin boy dreams of life.

The second selection is taken from the volume *Weep Before God*, published in 1962. It is a short, meditative poem which also relates to John Wain's father:

Anniversary

These are my thoughts on realising
That I am the same age as my father was
On the day I was born.

As a little scarlet howling mammal,
Crumpled and unformed, I depended entirely on someone
Not very different from what I am today.

When I think this over,
I feel more crumpled and unformed than ever:
I ask myself what I have done to compare with *that*.

It also makes me aware, inescapably,
Of having entered upon the high table-land,
The broad flat life of a mature man.

Where everything is seen from its actual distance,
E.g. childhood not so remote as to seem a boring myth,
Nor senility as something that awaits other people.

But deeper than that,
It is like entering a dark cone,
The shadow thrown across my life by the life it derives
    from.

And deeper than that still,
It is the knowledge that life is the one communicable thing.
It called. I heard it from where I slept in seed and liquid.

The patterns of seed and brine coalesced in a solemn dance,
Whence my life arose in the form of a crest,
And has carried itself blindly forward until now.

In ignorance of its uniqueness until now,
Until I stumbled over these thoughts solid as bricks,
And like bricks fearsome in their everyday squareness.

The third selection is also taken from *Weep Before God*. It is a
poem which stresses the sense of isolation experienced when one
contemplates the separateness of the unconscious mind of one's
closest intimates.

ANECDOTE OF 2 a.m.

"Why was she lost?" my darling said aloud
With never a movement in her sleep. I lay
Awake and watched her breathe, remote and proud.

Her words reached out where I could never be.
She dreamed a world remote from all I was.
"Why was she lost?" She was not asking me.

I knew that there was nothing I could say.
She breathed and dreamed beyond our kisses' sphere.
My watchful night was her unconscious day.

I could not tell what dreams disturbed her heart.
She spoke, and never knew my tongue was tied.
I longed to bless her but she lay apart.

That was our last night, if I could have known.
But I remember still how in the dark
She dreamed her question and we lay alone.

Biographical Note

John Wain was born at Stoke-on-Trent, in the centre of the urban area of North Staffordshire known as The Potteries, on 14 March 1925. He was educated at The High School, Newcastle-under-Lyme (an old-established market town on the western fringe of The Potteries) and at St John's College, Oxford.

He was Fereday Fellow at St John's College, from 1946 to 1949, and from 1947 to 1951 he was Lecturer in English Literature at the University of Reading. But his interest in writing prompted him to resign from full-time lecturing to become a freelance author and critic.

From 1953, when his first novel, *Hurry On Down*, appeared, John Wain has produced a large volume of writing, including novels, short stories, poems and literary criticism. Among his novels, *The Contenders* appeared in 1958, *Strike the Father Dead* in 1962, and *A Winter In the Hills* in 1970. Poetry has been published in *A Word Carved In a Sill* (1956), *Weep Before God* (1961), *Wildtrack* (1965), *Letters to Five Artists* (1969), and *The Shape of Feng* (1972). His critical writing has included *The Living World Of Shakespeare* (1964). His autobiography, *Sprightly Running* was published in 1962.

John Wain has, nevertheless, continued his involvement in academic work, and he has held some important lecturing posts. He was Churchill Visiting Professor at the University of Bristol in 1967, visiting Professor at the Centre Universitaire Experimentale de Vincennes, Paris, in 1969, and First Fellow in Creative Arts at Brasenose College, Oxford, during 1971 and 1972. In 1973 he was elected Professor of Poetry at Oxford University.

He lives quietly at Oxford and enjoys canoeing and walking.